THE NATURAL BEAUTY BOOK

Clare Maxwell-Hudson has also written

KALEIDOSCOPE OF BEAUTY (Octagon Press, 1968)

The NATURAL BEAUTY Book

a simple guide to do-it-yourself skin and body care

CLARE MAXWELL-HUDSON

Illustrations by Janina Ede

MACDONALD AND JANE'S · LONDON

First published in 1976 by
Macdonald and Jane's Publishers Limited,
Paulton House, 8 Shepherdess Walk, London N1

ISBN 0 356 08203 2

Printed in Great Britain by
REDWOOD BURN LIMITED
Trowbridge & Esher

CONTENTS

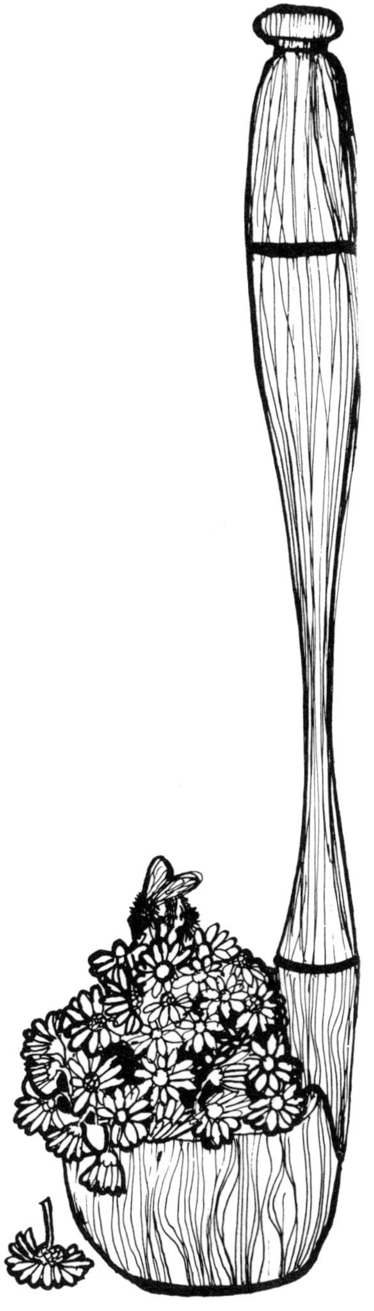

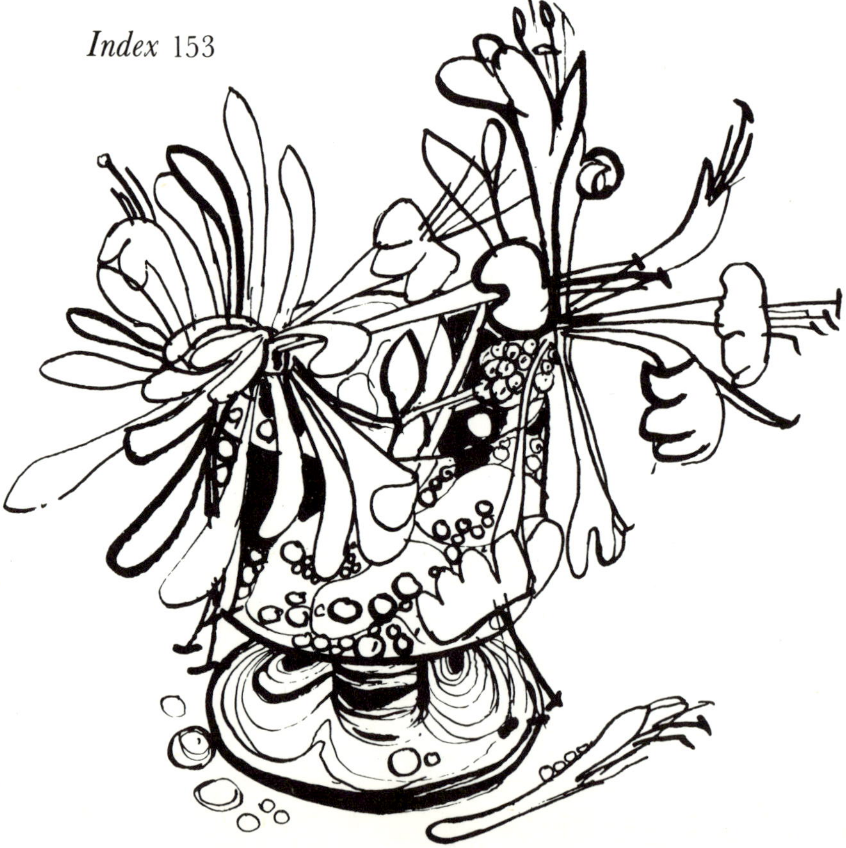

AUTHOR'S ACKNOWLEDGEMENTS

Grateful thanks for their encouragement and advice are offered to: Gote Andersson (Sweden), Major and Mrs R. Arliss, Michael Aspel, The BBC, Camilla Balmer (Argentine), the British Museum, Mrs Gilbert Brunsdon Lenaerts-Catoor (Belgium), Lady Olive Butler, Mrs Ian Byrne, Martin Callingham (Society of Cosmetic Chemists), Mme Chauvet (Cairo), Delia Collins, Fleur Cowles, Capitol Radio, Mme de Costa (Brazil), Victoria Davidson, Max Factor, Judy Graham, Dr Ensor Holiday, Joanna Halpin, Susan Hodgart, Faith Hornbacher (USA), Mrs Rachel and Louise Homan (Kenya), Mrs Eileen Kidd, Mrs Hyder-Nayssan (Afghanistan), Brigid Keenan (*Sunday Times*), Mrs Jasper Kettlewell, Peter Lacoux, Lancôme, Jane Lecomte, Anne MacDonald, Miles, Princess Helena Moutafian, Alberto Nino (Columbia), Robin Price (The Wellcome Library), Commander and Mrs M. Parry, Mrs David Perry, Mrs Rais (Fes), Ursula Rasica (Yugoslavia), Begum Kishwa Rizwi (Pakistan), The Sayeda Amina Ali-Shah, Gill Steuart, Thames Television, Sue Wallace, Pat Williams, Mrs J. Willemson (Greece), Sir Mortimer Wheeler, CH, KE, CIE, MC, TD, SPk, MA, DLit. FRS, FBA, FSA. I would also like to thank Janina Ede very much for the illustrations.

'Young ladies should take care of themselves. Young ladies are delicate plants. They should take care of their health and their complexion. My dear, did you change your stockings?'

Mr Woodhouse in *Emma*, Jane Austen

Pampering Yourself is Fun

HOW TO MAKE CREAMS

Making your own beauty preparations is as simple as basic cooking – sometimes simpler. Some books on this subject frighten people off by making things too complicated; some people never try making their own cosmetics because they think that commercial products must be better (they may get *that* idea just because they cost so much!).

This book has been written to show that both these ideas (that bought is best and cooking complicated) are fallacies. Making your own creams, tonics and lotions is *easy*. What is more, many recipes in this book could never be bought in the shops, because commercial firms would find the cost too high, and the shelf-life too short.

By learning to make your own cosmetics, you have at your fingertips not only more luxurious products than you could afford to buy, but also *more* of them. You can have a whole alchemist's shop in your house; ingredients (many already in your kitchen as you read this) waiting to be whipped up, sometimes within minutes, especially to suit *your* skin. For example, if you are tired one day you can use your 'invigorating beauty bath', and if you want to be consummately glamorous the next you can use your most exotic face mask. You would never have ten different *bought* masks, to do different jobs, on your dressing-table at once – but in your kitchen you can have twice as many waiting to be made up and put on.

Everything in this book has been tested both on myself and on friends and clients, and so I can vouch for the fact that all the recipes are delicious and extremely straightforward to make. They are so foolproof that I have even made some of them before the television cameras in a matter of minutes.

But putting creams on your skin is no substitute for the real basis of beauty, which is always – health. And the basis of good health is following a sensible diet and drinking lots of water (and I really mean *lots* – about eight glasses a day). Exercise is also important, so I have included some of my favourites for all parts of the body: efficient exercises, but not complicated or time-consuming. Massage can also play an important part in health and beauty, so I have included in this book various techniques for massaging yourself.

Wherever I have travelled, I have visited local health and beauty experts, and have always asked good-looking men and women about their beauty secrets; I have included the best of the ancient traditional secrets of Asia, Africa and Europe, and many that have never been written down before; and best of all, I've always been extremely lucky in that all over the world, people have been prepared to confide their beauty lore to me. Almost everything in this book is as applicable to men as women, and I think it's lovely to see that men are taking an interest in their appearance again. After all, history shows that they have nearly always been as vain as women!

Incidentally, you can save the price of this book on your first home-made pot of cream!

Creams, or emulsions, are all basically a mixture of water and oily substances, waxes and fragrances, in varying proportions. When reading this book you will notice that a lot of the creams seem very similar, that the same ingredients are used over and over again. But it is amazing how a slight change of the proportions can change the character of the cream so do be careful when measuring, otherwise you might find that the cream separates or just does not look as professional as it should. (In the list of ingredients for the individual recipes you will find that the oils and waxes are fractionally separated from the waters – which are also printed in italic type – and from the perfume, which should help prevent mistakes.) The majority of creams, also, are made basically in the same way, and so a general instructional note here would seem appropriate (although I do, in fact, repeat much of this in the individual recipes).

Have ready a bain marie or water bath, which can be made by using a large pan of some sort (a frying pan or roasting tin) filled with water. The separate enamel or pyrex bowls of oils and water are placed in this and the water bath is heated so that the contents of the bowls heat too, but very gently and slowly. This is because oils and waxes should never be exposed to direct heat as they can burn, and an intense heat can change the properties of the creams. The waters are heated simultaneously because they can thereby reach the same temperature as the oils. Keep the water in the water bath simmering, not boiling. When the oils and waxes have melted, remove both bowls from the heat and, stirring all the time, add the water to the waxes and oils. You can stir with either a wooden spoon or a glass rod, or you can use an electric beater on slow speed. Soon the cream will start to cool and thicken and now is the time to add colouring or perfume. (If your skin is sensitive or allergy prone, however, I would advise you to omit the perfume.) Continue stirring or beating until the cream is cool, then put it into jars and it is ready for use.

I am afraid you really do have to stir the creams, at least intermittently until they become cool; they tend to separate if you don't. However, if it does separate, don't worry; try beating it with an electric beater on low speed. You may be lucky, and the cream will emulsify. If it still doesn't gell, just re-melt it and start again. Oleic acid is a tremendous help here, as a couple of drops of this will usually bind together any cream or lotion which looks as though it will separate. I've also been told occasionally that creams have turned gritty. This can be either because the borax has not been properly dissolved, or because the cream was not

properly mixed.

Making creams is just like making mayonnaise. At first it requires tremendous concentration, but once you have mastered the art, it's easy. So persevere!

Jars and labelling

Keep any small bottles and jars with screw tops – medicine, spice or jam jars – and all those plastic and glass tubs and jars shop-bought creams come in. Ask your friends and neighbours, and soon you should have plenty.

Always label your jars, pots and bottles of creams *immediately*. I always think I'll remember what is in each container, but *never* do! So the moment you have put the top on the jar put a label on it. In fact if you want to be really efficient, keep a book and note down what you have made, when, how it turned out, and whether it suited your skin. This will save you a tremendous amount of time and is most useful and interesting to use.

Perfumes

Commercial products are frequently heavily perfumed, and it can be this perfume which causes, or at least contributes to, skin allergies. In most of our home-made creams I have included a few drops of perfume, but this is entirely optional, as they can irritate. I use essential oils to perfume most of my own creams; those I use most frequently are lemon verbena oil, jasmine oil, orange oil, rose oil and herb oils. After each recipe I have listed perfume (sometimes I specify a preference, sometimes not) as an ingredient. A few drops are all that is needed and – I repeat again – the addition is entirely optional.

You can use the following recipes – for rose and herb oils – for perfuming your creams or as delicious smelling body oil.

Herb oils

Essential oils can be bought from good herbalists, but it is great fun to experiment and make your own perfumed oils – and infinitely cheaper. Use any fresh herbs or flowers, either by themselves or in a mixture: thyme, rosemary, basil, lavender, rose petals, tarragon, marigolds or jasmine.

Crush the herbs in a pestle and mortar, put 2 tablespoons of the crushed herb into a half-pint bottle, and three quarters fill this with corn or sunflower oil and one tablespoon vinegar (or vodka). Cork the bottle and place in strong sunlight. Shake the bottle every time you pass it, or at least once a day. After a couple of weeks, strain the oil, and repeat with fresh herbs. If there is no strong sunlight, put the bottle in a double boiler, and gently heat. If you use a water bath, always keep the water below boiling point. Do this every day for a week, then strain and repeat the whole process. The oil is ready when it smells strongly of the herb.

I use these herb oils in my creams and lotions to perfume them. Also, as they are so cheap to make, you can use them really lavishly, and I use them for massage. I love them as they leave the body smelling so beautifully exotic.

Rose oil (how it was discovered)

While walking in the gardens of the palace at Agra (in India), Nur Jehan, 'Light of the World', discovered rose oil. Her women had put rose petals in a tank, and after being heated by the sun, these had given off an oily liquid with a delicious scent. Shah Jehan, 'King of the World' – whose devotion to his wife created the Taj Mahal – devised a means of collecting and bottling this liquid. The attar, or essential oil, was extracted by placing rose petals in a jar and covering them with water. These jars were capped and exposed to the sun. The attar congealed on the surface of the water, and was carefully skimmed off and used.

Nowadays, an infinitely more sophisticated method is employed, but it is a very costly business – literally thousands of rose petals are needed to make one ounce (28.3g) of essential oil. I

have made rose oil by using the old method, but needless to say it is not nearly as strongly perfumed as the bought product.

Preservatives

None of the creams in this book contain added preservatives, so do not get worried if one goes slightly rancid or grows a mould. Moulds flourish where there is access to air, so be sure to screw jars up tightly: a piece of foil or waxed paper can be placed on the surface of the cream to help prevent this. But remember that as these recipes contain natural ingredients this might occasionally happen, just as in jam, so don't worry. Most will keep perfectly for several months and their life can be lengthened by refrigeration. I keep a small jar in the bathroom and the rest in the refrigerator. One friend became so enthusiastic about making her own creams that she had a tiny refrigerator fitted into her dressing-room so that all her creams were kept perfect and were always near at hand, ready for use.

There is one preservative that I have found effective called Nipagin M. When heating the water for your cream add a couple of drops of Nipagin M. Stir constantly until the oily globules disperse then proceed with the recipe. With the addition of this your cream will have a longer shelf life. However, the idea of making your own creams and lotions is not to keep them forever, but to make small batches and to use them lavishly while they are still fresh. Cream kept in a jar, however pretty it might look, isn't going to do you any good: so use it and enjoy it!

Equipment

Enamel or pyrex bowls.
One large frying pan (or roasting tin).
Metal measuring spoons. Plastic ones can be used, but they tend to break – and melt – so try and get metal ones.
A set of measuring cups. These are not absolutely essential but make life much easier.
An electric beater. Again not essential but a great asset.
You can use a *wooden spoon* or *glass rod* instead but it involves much more work.
A *liquidizer* or a good strong *sieve.*
A pipette or eyedropper, for adding the perfume.
A roll of kitchen paper is invaluable for wiping jars, spoons, hands, etc.
Jars and bottles to put the creams into.
Labels, so that you can instantly stick a label on every pot of cream or lotion.

Where to buy ingredients

Most of the ingredients used in this book are readily available from a good chemist or health shop.

Waxes

Beeswax, emulsifying wax and cocoa butter can be ordered through the chemist, although you may have to buy rather a large quantity. You could, of course, share with a friend, but as these are the basic ingredients of so many creams and don't go bad, you can always quite happily keep a stock of them.

Lanolin

This is readily available from the chemist. There are two types of lanolin: anhydrous which has no added water, and hydrous which has a fairly large water content. I recommend the use of anhydrous in these creams. If, however, you have inadvertently bought the wrong one, don't worry: use it but add less water to the cream. As an experiment buy a small pot of each and see the difference it makes to the cream; the one with the anhydrous will be much richer and greasier.

Oils

These are readily available from health food shops or large chemists. For essential oils either order them from your local chemist, or from Baldwin's, 77 Walworth Road, London SE 17.

Herbs, spices, powders, brans etc

The other ingredients, camphor BP, Fuller's Earth, tincture of benzoin etc., can always be ordered from a good chemist. And the herbs, brans, lentils, vitamin pills are all available from health food shops.

For any unusual herb or spice I have always eventually found them at one of these well-stocked shops:

Culpeper's, Bruton Street, London W1;
Robert Jackson's, Piccadilly, London W1;
Cranks, Marshall Street, London W1.

And if you are having trouble obtaining anything at all through your local chemist, I have always found that John Bell & Croydon have been able to help: even when I was making up old-fashioned, unuseable cosmetics for an exhibition, they somehow managed to obtain the most extraordinary ingredients for me:

John Bell & Croydon, Wigmore Street, London W1.

Notes on quantities

The following rough equivalents have proved useful to me:

60 drops	1 teaspoon
3 teaspoons	1 tablespoon
2 tablespoons	⅛ cup = 1 fl. oz.
4 tablespoons	¼ cup = 2 fl. oz.
8 tablespoons	½ cup = 4 fl. oz.
12 tablespoons	¾ cup = 6 fl. oz.
16 tablespoons	1 cup = 8 fl. oz.
32 tablespoons	2 cups = 16 fl. oz.

Since volume and weight are different measurements it is not possible to render the one in terms of the other in a simple table of equivalents, because bulk and weight do not correspond for all substances. In the case of oil, in fact, the same oil of different grades may have different weights.

60 drops	5 ml = 1 teaspoon
1000 mls	1 litre
1 litre	1.759 pints
1 pint	20 fl. oz. = 0.568 litres

weights

15.4 grains	1 gm.
28.3 gms	1 oz.
16 ozs.	1 lb.
1 lb.	0.453 kilogms.
1 kilogm.	2.20 lbs.

'So white is her face that when you admire such perfection you see your own visage submerged in her clarity.'

Ibn Abd Rabbihi from Cordoba, AD 860-940

The Face and Head

THE SKIN AND ITS CARE

Introduction

We all have different attitudes towards skin (a physiologist, for instance, thinks of it as an outer layer which weighs about six pounds and covers roughly seventeen square feet!). We don't have to be quite so brutally basic, but even a general knowledge of the skin, and its care, is far better than romantic illusions about it.

The skin consists of layers. The outer layer, the epidermis, is a mass of cells in two levels, the lower level of which is living, and the upper dead. The outermost level – the dead scales – is the one with which we are usually working. I sometimes think of this as very fine leather: leather which is looked after and properly treated looks better and lasts longer than if it is neglected. Beneath the epidermis we have the dermis, which is a jelly-like substance supported by bundles of collagen fibres, and below this there is a layer of fat (there is generally more fat in female skin and it is this which gives a soft, rounded look to the body).

Skin is not simply a waterproof wrapping: it is a highly efficient organ which fulfills many functions. It protects the body from bacteria, it eliminates waste matter, and it breathes. Because skin is to some extent self-cleaning and self-lubricating, we are too inclined to let it do these jobs by itself. The sebaceous glands, which produce sebum (oil) keep the skin supple, but not everyone can rely on them to operate properly. Sometimes they over-produce giving us greasy skin, and sometimes under-produce, giving us dry skin. This is why we have to help the skin along a little with cosmetics, to rectify these imbalances.

Almost everything about the skin is connected with health and beauty. Thousands of tiny nerve-endings provide us with our sense of touch, and other disturbances of the skin's functioning. The performance of the skin, in controlling water loss and in regulating your temperature, is directly related to your health. The skin is one of the greatest indicators of good or bad health,

both physical and emotional.

Diet is also of vital importance, and no skin can be at its best without proper nutrition. Try to avoid too many carbohydrates, particularly sugar, which tend to give the skin a pasty look. Instead eat plenty of fresh fruit and vegetables and, as your skin is protein, fish, nuts and meat. The rule where food is concerned is the plainer the better. If you want a good skin keep away from those rich sauces and cream cakes! You are what you eat!

Your skin needs vitamins, and will normally get sufficient in a balanced diet. Vitamin A aids the circulation, and a lack of it is thought to show drying, scaliness and a weakness of the epidermis. Vitamin B, especially yeast, is recommended by many dieticians to clear the skin of spots and as an aid to healthy hair. Vitamin C is necessary to maintain the tiny blood-vessels in the skin, to prevent scurvy and bleeding gums. Vitamin E, the fertility vitamin, is widely believed to make the skin appear more youthful, and to assist in the mending of scar tissue. The skin also produces Vitamin D through the action of sunlight upon it.

Exercise of any sort – bicycling, walking and swimming – improves the circulation. As it is the blood which feeds the skin, any increase in blood circulation will keep it healthy. One marvellous way to increase the circulation to one's face and scalp is by doing headstands. If only we could do some sort of exercise each day, we would not only improve our bodies but also our skin.

Drinking water is another easy way of improving your complexion. I am a great believer in drinking a lot of water, at least eight glasses a day. It helps to clean the system of impurities, making the skin healthy and eyes bright and shiny. Try not to drink with your meals, though, as this may cause indigestion. Enough sleep is another very important beauty aid. You only have to look at yourself when you'rc tired; without sleep your skin is pale and dead-looking.

The skin also has an ability for absorption, which is why we use creams to moisturize and lubricate. The oils and water of these creams usually lubricate the upper superficial layer of the skin only, but a little can be absorbed into the living cells which helps to keep the skin moist and supple.

Your skin type

An easy way to discover what type of skin you have, is to wipe your face with a dry tissue first thing in the morning. If there is oil on it, you have a greasy skin; if you only have grease in the centre panel, then you have a combination skin. If there is no grease on the tissue at all, you have either a dry or normal skin. Find out which by washing with soap and water. If your skin is left feeling stretched too tight, shiny and parched, it is dry. If it feels smooth, supple and elastic, it is normal.

Until recently men have considered it slightly effeminate to look after their skin, but thank goodness things have changed and now they are taking care of themselves. Most of these recipes for skin care are suitable for both men and women.

With each skin type I have suggested ways in which to look after it, but remember that your skin is constantly changing so vary the use of your cosmetics to suit your requirements. Although you might have a greasy skin, it will sometimes benefit from a recipe for dry skin, and vice-versa. Experiment and see what suits you and what your skin needs *now*!

An Ideal Normal Skin
A healthy, normal skin is unblemished, velvety smooth and supple. It appears satiny, and the light should penetrate and bounce back, giving it a translucent quality. This is the ideal we would all like to achieve, and if you are lucky enough to have this type of skin, look after it and keep it that way.

cleansing In the morning wash either with plain water, soap and water, face-washing grains or rosewater. In the evening take off your make-up with cleansing cream, then remove the traces of grease with a mild skin tonic.

moisturizing Always use a moisturizer in the day, either under your make-up or, as your skin is so lovely, instead of it.

nourishing Your skin will benefit by occasional nourishing. How often you use a rich cream depends on your particular skin.

Dry Skin
A dry skin seems to be drawn too tightly over the bones. It is fine-textured and feels parched, and has a tendency to broken veins, flakiness and dry patches. Tiny lines are normally visible which, if neglected, turn into wrinkles and lines – and so a dry skin needs lots of pampering. The oil glands are not supplying enough lubrication to the skin, and without this protection the skin becomes dehydrated. First check your diet, do you eat

enough fat and proteins? If your skin is really dry, take a course of cod liver oil tablets. Don't be put off by the sound of this as it really is *most* effective.

cleansing This is best done with a cream, followed by a very mild tonic like rosewater or a herbal infusion to remove the remaining traces of oil, and to leave the skin feeling fresh. Whether you use a skin tonic or not is purely a question of personal preference. Be careful, however, not to use a strong one, as anything containing alcohol will dry out the skin.

washing Some people with dry skin never wash their faces, but I think it is good to have an occasional real soap and water scrub. If you are afraid it will over-dry your skin, use lots of moisturizer afterwards. Try washing with milk or, if you are feeling extravagant, white wine. Instead of soap, use oatmeal or almond meal which are much less drying than soap.

moisturizing Lubricating and feeding are essential for your type of skin, and you should no more think of going out without a moisturizer than you would without your clothes. At night, or if your skin is feeling particularly dry, restore it with a rich nourishing cream. Put this on in the bath, or at least twenty minutes before getting into bed, then blot off the excess. Your skin will have absorbed all the cream it can in ten minutes, and so any excess will only block the pores, prevent the skin from breathing, and make your pillows dirty.

Greasy skin

A greasy skin looks shiny, thick, slightly toneless and dull coloured, and often has blackheads. The sebaceous glands are working overtime and producing more oil than is needed, thus making the face greasy, and coarsening and enlarging the pores.

cleansing Greasy skin requires more cleansing than other skins. Grease tends to pick up dirt and grime which clog the pores and produce blackheads. So be meticulous about cleansing. In the morning wash with soap and water, and again at midday if you have time. In the evening remove any make-up with cleansing cream, but be sure to remove all traces of oil, either by washing again or by using a skin tonic.

toning This is imperative for greasy skin as it tends to be sluggish, and the toning will improve the circulation, bring colour and blood to the skin, and improve the texture. (But don't over-dry the skin by using astringents which are too strong.) Use the cotton-wool patters I describe in the toning section (p.36).

moisturizing This is not always necessary as oily skin provides its own protective lubrication but this will depend on your particular skin. Personally I am in favour of using a non-greasy moisturizer in the day, but no night creams, as I feel that even oily skin needs the added moisture. But you must find out what *your* skin needs, as each skin is individual and reacts slightly differently.

Combination Skin

This skin type – dry cheeks and a greasy centre panel – is very common. Treat your skin as two individual skins. Cleanse the centre panel with an astringent or strong skin tonic, followed by no cream at all, or just a light moisturizer. The cheeks need to be treated as you would treat dry skin, so pamper them with lots of moisturizers and skin food. When giving yourself a mask – use two, one suitable for each area.

Cleansing

The basis of beauty is a good skin, and the secret of a good skin is keeping it clean. There are three methods of doing this: steaming (which is the most thorough), washing, and using creams and lotions.

Steaming

This thorough, deep-cleansing method is beneficial to all types of skin. It cleans the skin of all surface dirt, stimulates the circulation, and unclogs blocked pores. It can be used every day if you have a very greasy skin, but normally once a week would be sufficient (slightly less if your skin is very dry).

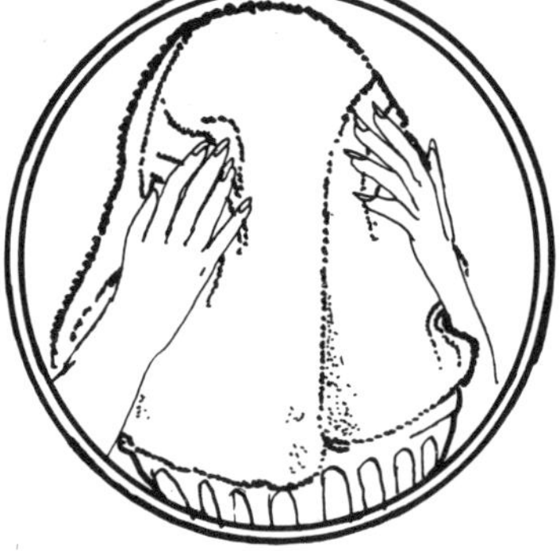

Lean over a large bowl of boiling water, and cover your head with a towel, making a tent around the bowl. The steam will open the pores, loosen blackheads and bring spots to a head. Do not get too close to the water – twelve to twenty-four inches is near enough – for if the steam is too hot it might cause broken veins. To make this steaming even more beneficial, add a tablespoon of herbs to the water; elderflower and camomile are the old favourites for this, but also try lavender, thyme and rosemary for a stimulating cleanse, and comfrey and fennel for healing. These herbs make this a real luxury treatment as they smell so delicious.

Steam your face for about ten to twenty minutes, and if you have any blackheads which you just cannot resist, now is the time to extract them. But be meticulous about it, using a fresh piece of cotton wool for each one, and dabbing each with an astringent tonic afterwards. Now rinse your face with a skin tonic, and apply a suitable mask, to close the pores and tighten the skin. If you have been extracting blackheads, use a mask containing yoghourt, kaolin, cucumber or comfrey, as these are astringent and healing.

If you suffer from pustular acne I would not advise steaming, as the steam and heat can spread the infection. Try and get professional advice from your doctor or beautician.

Washing

There is still controversy about whether to wash or not. The superstition that soap and water are bad for the skin probably arose in the days when soaps were very alkaline and did tend to dry and irritate the skin. Nowadays this no longer applies, as modern soaps often have lanolin and other oils added to them to counteract this drying effect. A leading London dermatologist told me that he is always having to 'prescribe' washing to his patients. Skin needs to be free from all oils and grease sometimes to allow it to breathe and for it to stabilize itself.

We are always hearing of the old woman who has beautiful skin and uses only soap and water. Recently I met such a woman – an Argentinian of eighty years old – and her skin was remarkable. She felt sure her skin was so good because she not only washed it often but did exercises each morning, thus stimulating the blood supply to the skin and feeding it. Of course this treatment would not suit everyone, but don't be afraid of soap and water – try it and see whether it is suitable for you or not.

Lily Langtry the 'Jersey Lily', who had a lovely complexion and was so admired by the Prince of Wales, later Edward VII, always washed in rainwater. Next time it rains why not put a bowl outside and try it – rainwater is beautifully soft. If there is none available try using bottled spring water or simply add a teaspoon of sodium sesqui carbonate to your washing water to soften it. Diane de Poitiers, the mistress of Henry II, was said to have had a flawless complexion at the age of sixty, and her peerless beauty has been attributed to the constant use of cold water for washing.

I think one of the most invaluable aids to a good skin is a

complexion brush (a natural bristle brush or a soft rubber complexion brush). If you cannot find one of these, use a soft, new nail brush, soap the face and scrub. Use a small, circular movement concentrating on the nose and chin areas. The scrubbing stimulates the skin, brings the blood to the surface, removes dead cells, unclogs pores, and leaves the skin feeling beautifully smooth and clean.

oatmeal scrub If you do not have a complexion brush try washing with finely ground oatmeal (available from any health food shop). This is slightly abrasive and very cleansing. I keep a little pot next to the soap by the basin so that it is always ready for use. Take a little, roughly a teaspoon, in the palm of your hand, mix with a little water, and use the paste to wash with. Or better still, make up the following:

special oatmeal scrub Mix together and use to wash with as above. The orange peel must be one of the easiest and cheapest ingredients possible. Every time you eat an orange simply keep the peel and dry it – on the windowsill, on your storage heater, in the sun or in a slow oven – and then grind it up in a coffee grinder or a pestle and mortar. Sieve it before use. I heard of this exotic use of orange peel in Kashmir where the women have marvellous complexions.

- 1 tablespoon finely-ground oatmeal
- 1 tablespoon finely-ground orange peel
- 1 tablespoon ground almonds

amazing Brazilian washing secret Soap your face well, adding a small handful of sugar to the lather. Massage this in for a couple of minutes and then rinse off with warm water, and if you have spots use lemon juice for the final rinse.

This is one of my favourite recipes. If your skin feels grubby and grimy or if it is looking spotty and sluggish washing with sugar for a few days shows a remarkable improvement. A schoolboy I know used this at boarding school and it cured his spotty skin without anyone realizing he was doing anything as effeminate as trying to improve his complexion.

a Greek counterpart This recipe uses the same ingredients with the addition of an egg yolk, and is less abrasive as it has been cooked. The addition of the yolk also makes it ideal for slightly dry skin. It was given to me by a beautiful Greek woman from Crete whose grandmother always used it.

Put 1½ tablespoonfuls of sugar with ½ tablespoonful of water in a pan over a low heat. When it begins to caramel, remove from the heat and add a beaten egg yolk. Replace on the heat for a minute and mix in several drops of lemon juice. When cool enough, make into tiny balls and store in a jar to use either in your washing water or, moistened, as a mask.

variations The water left over from cooking your vegetables makes vitamin-filled face-washing liquid (cabbage, spinach or bean juice) which should be used quickly while still fresh.

Ann Boleyn is said to have not only used wine to wash her face, but also in her bath (which was then quaffed by the court nobles). This is an extravagant prescription for a good skin, but the Scandinavians are more down to earth and use beer foam to wash with, as do some Uruguayans. A friend of mine, visiting Uruguay, noticed that many women had marvellous complexions, and was told that they used the sediments from the beer factory to wash in and it was this that kept their skins blemish-free.

Cleansing creams

These are especially designed not only to lift the dirt and grime from the skin, but also to remove make-up. Make-up has a waxy base which cannot be properly penetrated and cleansed by simply using soap and water, and a cleansing cream or lotion is essential for this. Cleansers should be applied with an upward movement, and kept on the skin for about half a minute, so that they can actually dissolve the make-up. Then remove with either a tissue or some damp cotton wool.

It is a great temptation when one is tired to go to bed without removing make-up. Make it a golden rule never to do this; stale make-up and the day's dirt and grime not only clog the pores causing blackheads, but will eventually coarsen the skin. So, no matter what type of skin you have, and whether you wear make-up or not, you need a cleansing cream.

easy cleansing cream You can make this cream in just a few minutes – in fact I made it in front of TV cameras once in less than ten minutes.

½ tablespoon beeswax
1 tablespoon emulsifying wax
4 tablespoons baby oil
2 tablespoons coconut oil

2 tablespoons water
¼ teaspoon borax
1 tablespoon witch-hazel

perfume (a few drops of essential oil)

Measure the waxes and oils into an enamel bowl and melt slowly in a pan of boiling water. In a separate bowl heat the water and borax until the borax is throughly dissolved, then add the witch-hazel, being careful not to leave it on the heat too long or the latter will evaporate. When the waxes are melted, remove both bowls from the heat and mix in the waters, beating (or stirring) all the time. When the cream is beginning to cool, add the perfume – lemon verbena oil is lovely and fresh for a cleanser. Beat until the mixture thickens and cools and soon you will have half a cup of delicious light cream. In this recipe we use baby oil, which is a mineral oil, because it does not penetrate the skin, it is easy to work with, spreads easily and liquifies readily – and it is very inexpensive. All of these qualities make it ideal for use in a cleansing cream.

Galen's rose cleansing cream Over 1,700 years ago Galen, a Greek physician, made the very first cream of which we have a record. The ingredients included white wax, spermaceti, almond oil, rosewater and borax. Instead of spermaceti – a wax obtained from the sperm oil of whales – we use emulsifying wax which is much more efficient, humane and cheaper. And we also use mineral oil rather than almond oil as it is much cheaper and cannot be absorbed by the skin.

As you can see, the basic ingredients of our creams haven't changed that much since Galen's day, and are just as beneficial to us as they have been to women for the last 1,700 years. My version of the cream is slightly changed, but is still a simple recipe, using the best ingredients.

1½ tablespoons beeswax (or white paraffin wax)
1 tablespoon emulsifying wax
4 tablespoons mineral oil

6 tablespoons rosewater
½ teaspoon borax

perfume (rose oil)

Melt the waxes and oil together, and at the same time heat the water and borax, making sure that the borax is completely dissolved. Remove both bowls from the heat and quickly stir the water into the oil, beating continuously. A white cream will start to form, and when the mixture begins to cool, add a drop of rose oil. Carry on beating until the cream is really cool, and you will have made about a cup of delicious, soft cleansing cream.

3 teaspoons beeswax
4 teaspoons coconut oil
5 teaspoons mineral oil or olive oil

4 tablespoons cucumber juice
1 teaspoon glycerine
pinch borax

1 drop green colouring

cucumber cleansing cream Melt the oils and wax in the usual way over a pan of boiling water. At the same time in a separate bowl, heat the cucumber juice, glycerine, colouring and borax, ensuring that the borax dissolves completely. (To make the cucumber juice use quarter of a cucumber, liquidized and strained; if you don't have a liquidizer mash the cucumber and then sieve it.) When the contents of both bowlfuls are melted and warm add the water drop by drop to the oil stirring all the time. Now remove from the heat, and stir or beat until the mixture is cool. This makes about half a cup of lovely soft cream. It melts on touching the skin, efficiently easing away the dirt. Cucumber juice goes bad very quickly, so do keep it in the refrigerator. You can, of course, make this recipe using ordinary water, which means that it will keep; but I love it with the cucumber as it is such a thorough cleanser and smells so fresh. So make little batches, use it often, and do not give it a chance to go off.

Remember to label it!

2 tablespoons vegetable lard
2 tablespoons corn oil
4 tablespoons sunflower oil

perfume

simple country cleansing cream This is a very quick cream to make. Simply melt the lard and mix in the oils; stir, cool and perfume – and there you are, about half a cup of pale golden cream. Nothing could be easier and it works.

violet cleansing cream A medieval bishop wrote: 'Of all the fragrant herbs none can compete with the purple violet.' As we use cleansing cream each day I thought we could enjoy this lovely fragrance by using it in this cream.

½ tablespoon lanolin
1 tablespoon petroleum jelly
4 tablespoons mineral oil

10 tablespoons water

5 drops violet extract

Melt the oils and heat the water, and then mix together slowly, stirring all the time. Remove from the heat, and continue to beat together. In just a few minutes you will have made about a cup of fairly thin, pure white cleansing cream. It feels very fine, and being quite liquid, can also be used as a body lotion.

Masks

Masks are a marvellous way to pamper yourself, as well as being one of the oldest known forms of beautifying treatment. You put on a preparation, leave it for ten to twenty minutes, then wash it off. There are many different types of mask: some act as a quick pick-me-up; some have nourishing, healing or cleansing actions, some whip up the circulation, and some have an astringent action, temporarily ironing out wrinkles. Unfortunately, masks cannot perform miracles, but they do always freshen the skin, and leave it soft and glowing. They can be used every day, once a week, or just when you feel your skin needs a boost. They are a useful addition to your regular skin care, and should be enjoyed.

Everything in your kitchen (well, *nearly* everything) could be helping you to look beautiful. If you can eat it, the likelihood is that you can put it on your face – fruit juices, honey, brans, eggs, vegetables and oatmeal, for instance. The recipes I give are examples, but the ideal is to experiment and find the ones that suit *your* skin the most. I have put the mask recipes throughout the book into cleansing, toning and nourishing sections, but these obviously overlap. So start experimenting, and pamper and

amuse yourself.

One of the most important things to remember when using a mask, is to *relax*. Allow yourself ten to fifteen minutes, lie with your feet above your head, put on eyepads, and relax.

milk mask One of the simplest – and probably cheapest – masks is milk. Damp some cotton wool with milk, and cleanse your face with it. The skin can benefit enormously from a quick cleanse during the day, and the full joy of this milk mask is that it is invisible, and could even be left on throughout lunch or an afternoon at the office without anyone knowing.

miraculous cleansing mask Mix thoroughly into a paste, apply and leave on for fifteen minutes. This is one of the very best cleansing masks. The brewers' yeast stimulates the flow of blood to the skin, this nourishes it, helps healing and gives the complexion a healthy glow. (Incidentally, brewers' yeast is also marvellous for the skin when taken internally.) The yoghourt cleanses thoroughly, and the vegetable and fruit provide vitamins and minerals.

1 tablespoon powdered brewers' yeast
½ tablespoon yoghourt
1 teaspoon lemon juice
1 teaspoon orange juice
1 teaspoon carrot juice
1 teaspoon olive oil

This mask is suitable for all skin types, particularly if they feel and look sluggish or spotty (if your skin is very dry add more oil, and if very oily, leave it out). I always use this mask in winter when everyone's skin has that grey, tired look: after a few applications the complexion looks alive and glowing again.

a simpler version Mix and apply as above. Natural yoghourt by itself is a thorough cleanser, and so this combination is really effective.

1 teaspoon yeast
1 teaspoon oatmeal
1 tablespoon yoghourt

One word of warning: yeast activates the skin so that it can bring out impurities (i.e. spots), so do not use it immediately before a party unless you have tried it before, and know how it reacts on your skin.

Lots of men I know use this as it is simple to make and yet so successful.

buttermilk cleansing mask Heat a cup of buttermilk and put into it 3 tablespoons of elderflower blossoms. Simmer on a very low heat for about half an hour; take it off the heat, leave it to cool, and use as a face mask.

Buttermilk makes a marvellous cleanser, as it helps to refine large pores. Both buttermilk and elderflowers are renowned for their bleaching and cleansing properties, so that the combination makes a truly effective cleanser.

meal masks Roman women were extremely interested in cosmetics, and used to apply a paste of barley meal, pea-flower and water. They left it on for several hours in order to make their skin soft and supple. In a poem Juvenal alludes to this treatment:

> Th' eclipse then vanishes and all her face
> Is opened and restored to every grace;
> The crust removed, her cheeks as smooth as silk
> Are polished with a wash of asses' milk.

Asses' milk might be a trifle difficult to obtain, but try washing the mask off with cows' milk.

The following meal mask, using finely ground oatmeal, has always been a great favourite of mine. A Columbian friend in her thirties, who is always being taken for a teenager, uses this mask each morning.

1 tablespoon finely-ground oatmeal
1 tablespoon milk
Few drops of almond oil

Mix these into a paste and apply to a clean face. Leave it on for fifteen minutes, then rinse off. Another version is to mix the oatmeal with buttermilk or yoghourt instead of milk.

1 carrot
1 turnip

carrot and turnip mask Boil the carrot and turnip and mash them into a paste. Apply for 10 minutes and rinse off with milk. This recipe is used by the famous Hungarian dermatologist, Dr Erno Laszlo; he has a large clinic in New York which is attended by the most famous women of the world, and he always advocates the use of fruit and vegetable juices on the skin. Many of my clients go to him when in New York, and always use his soaps. I am told he believes in washing the skin, and suggests washing the face at least once a day, in either milk for dry skin or cucumber juice for greasy skin.

This carrot and turnip mask leaves the skin feeling beautifully fresh and clean. Carrots are rich in Vitamin A, which is most beneficial in treating the skin and is thought to help irritated skin, and turnips (like potatoes) are marvellous cleansers.

2 tablespoons dried orange peel (see p. 29)
2 teaspoons chick-pea flour (or oatmeal)
2 tablespoons cream

Kashmiri face mask Mix into a paste and apply generously all over the face and neck. After 10 or 15 minutes, when it is dry, rub it off using an upward circular motion – this abrasive action smoothes and cleans the skin. This is one of my favourites of the moment as it smells so good, and I love the thought that this recipe must have been used for thousands of years. It will suit all skin types; and is a most effective cleanser, making the skin feel smooth and satiny.

potato cleanser Another easy way to clean the face is simply by rubbing it over with a raw potato. There isn't any excuse not to try this: surely you have one in the kitchen and you can try it right away! Potatoes contain Vitamin C, and they thoroughly cleanse the skin of blemishes and are even reputed to benefit eczema.

If you have a juice extractor you could make up this mask: it is marvellous for greasy, spotty skins, as the Fuller's Earth seems to absorb all the dirt and grease from the skin.

1 tablespoon potato juice
1 tablespoon Fuller's Earth

Potato juice is also well known as a cure for constipation; if you take half a glassful each morning, I believe the results are amazing!

East African paw-paw mask The paw-paw, also known as the papaya, contains an enzyme which literally eats away the dead cells that accumulate on the skin's surface. In Kenya, we used to marinate very tough meat in paw-paw to tenderize it – it does the same to our skin, cleaning it, and leaving it fresh and rejuvenated.

An African friend told me this method of using paw-paw. Mash two tablespoons of ripe paw-paw flesh and spread over a clean face. Rinse off after ten to fifteen minutes with warm water. When I am at home in Kenya, after breakfasting on paw-paw, I rub the inside of the skin of the fruit over my face. In this way I give myself a daily mini-mask, and after a few days the improvement is remarkable and my skin glows with health.

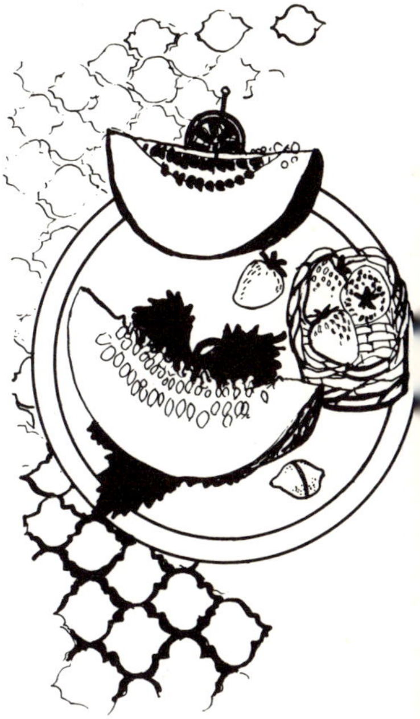

water melon juice This acts as a deep cleanser and skin tightener. It is particularly good for dry, horny skin, and is said to abolish wrinkles.

extravagant and most luxurious cleansing masks Mash up 3 large strawberries, apply as a mask and leave on for 10 minutes. Wash off with rosewater. Strawberries are slightly acidic, containing Vitamin C. They cleanse the skin thoroughly, leaving it sparklingly clean. In fact Nero's wife, Poppaea, is said to have bathed in strawberries (if we cannot afford to do that, we can at least use this mask).

An equally luxurious, more alcoholic, recipe consists of mashing and sieving the flesh of half a peach; and mixing it with a tablespoon of brandy. If you can refrain from eating this, it is a marvellously refreshing mask. Tinned peaches can be used just as effectively.

Toning

Basically skin tonics freshen the skin, but they also continue the cleansing process by removing all residual grease. The cheapest toner is simply to splash your face with cold water. Skin tonics are generally composed of infusions of herbs, flowers, vinegars, rosewater, orange-flower water or witch-hazel, which is slightly astringent, and sometimes small amounts of glycerine. They are suitable for dry or normal skins. Stronger skin tonics, or astringents, again contain infusions and distilled water, but have in them larger amounts of witch-hazel and/or alcohol. They dry the skin, the alcohol removing any trace of oil which was on the skin, and are therefore suitable for greasy skins. But if you like the sound of a recipe for an astringent, and your skin is dry; simply cut down the alcohol content and use it. Personally, I am against very strong astringents for any skin, as I feel the harsh action of the alcohol toughens and coarsens the skin and prevents it from functioning normally.

Most of the recipes in this section make excellent pre-shaves and after-shaves which are, after all, only glorified skin tonics.

Normally you would stroke on your tonic or astringent with a piece of cotton wool, but if your skin is looking sluggish, give it a salon treatment and pat it on with a brisk slapping movement. Toning like this stimulates the blood supply to the skin, thus enabling the natural restorative function of the skin to take place by feeding the cells (like our headstands bringing the blood to the face).

Make a 'patter' out of a 4-inch square of damp cotton wool, fold over the left corner then wrap this with the right corner and there you are. Moisten it with your skin tonic and pat on. The neck and chin benefit especially from this, but avoid any areas with broken veins, so go easy on the cheeks.

Skin Tonics

rosewater One of the oldest, best skin-fresheners is rosewater. It is said to have been discovered by an Arabian doctor, Avicenna, in the tenth century. He invented the means of distillation, and did his first experiments with rose petals, thus producing rosewater. This rosewater soon became so popular that when Saladin entered Jerusalem in 1187, he had the floors and walls of the mosque washed with it. When the noblemen returned from Palestine after the Crusades they brought with them rosewater, as well as the custom of offering it as washing water after a meal (very necessary, as they did not use forks!). The custom of sprinkling rosewater on the hands of guests when entering a home is still prevalent all over the Middle East as a token of welcome.

Rosewater is available from most chemists, but it is very easy to make your own.

4½ l (1 gallon) purified water
2 tablespoons essence of roses

Mix the rose essence into the water and shake thoroughly. This is much cheaper than buying it and so you can afford to be really generous with it – wash your hands in it, add it to the bath water, use it as your final hair rinse, use it in your creams by replacing water with rosewater. You will find it cropping up again and again in this book. So make some now and use it lavishly.

gypsy rosewater A gypsy told me that her mother always made her own rosewater, and here is her recipe. Take 2 handfuls of dark, scented rose petals and put them into a jar or wide-topped bottle. Cover them with 1 litre (1¾ pints) of water and half a pound of sugar. Firmly close the top and shake vigorously. Steep this mixture for two hours, shake again, then strain and store it in a cold place. To make the water smell even more, refill the jar with fresh rose petals, and repeat the process until the water smells as strong as you want it.

rosewater and witch-hazel tonic This is probably the most famous skin tonic of all. Its fame is well deserved, mixing the fragrant rosewater with healing witch-hazel. In Brazil witch-hazel is known as the 'miraculous cure'. It is used as an antiseptic, to reduce swellings and puffiness, and as a skin tightener. All over Europe, witch-hazel has enjoyed the same popularity, and it is used a great deal in homeopathic treatments. To make this lotion simply mix ¾ cup rosewater and ¼ cup witch-hazel. If you have a very greasy skin you can use equal proportions of rosewater and witch-hazel.

flower and herb waters Flower and herb waters of all kinds make deliciously scented, highly effective skin tonics. They have restorative, soothing and cleansing properties.

The basic recipe is 2 tablespoons of dried herbs or flowers, or approximately 3 handfuls of fresh ones to a pint of water. Pour the boiling water over the herbs, and cover; this prevents any goodness being lost with the steam. Let the herbs steep for at least twenty minutes, but a couple of hours is better. Strain and bottle.

marigold skin tonic Marigolds are well known for their healing properties: use either the fresh or dried flowers to make this skin tonic, following the method given above for flower and herb waters. To ensure a supply throughout the year pick the flowers when they are at their peak, and dry them in an airing cupboard or similar dark, dry place. Dry a large batch and store them in glass jars. Use the simple marigold water either by itself, or mixed with 2 tablespoons of witch-hazel, as a skin tonic. It is especially good for greasy, spotty skin. Marigolds were also widely used in old-fashioned face creams, and so you can try replacing some of the water in your favourite recipe with some marigold water.

hollyhock skin tonic In summer hollyhocks are prolific in most parts of the country, so why not try this recipe. Put 3 to 4 tablespoons of hollyhock leaves into half a pint of boiling water, cover and simmer gently for five minutes. Leave to stand for 20 minutes, then strain and it's ready for use. The hollyhock possesses valuable soothing properties, and is greatly used by the Bedouin Arabs, both internally to soothe the digestion, and externally to soothe inflamed skin.

Many other flowers and leaves can be used in the same way: *Lilac* and *Geranium* for their antiseptic properties; *Lily of the Valley* leaves are used for cooling inflammations; *Honeysuckle* promotes healing; *Lime Flowers* make a good cleanser; *Lavender* has a calmative value as well as a delicious fresh smell and *Dandelions* are reputed to cure sallowness of the skin.

elderflower water Elderflower water has a refining effect on the skin, and in the last century it was used to keep skin blemish-free and delicate looking. It is also soothing and healing, for an Irishwoman told me once that when she had nothing to soothe her wind and sun burns, she applied an infusion of elderflowers, which helped most effectively. To make it, gather several stalks (a large handful) of the fresh elderflowers, wash them and put about 6 tablespoonfuls into a large jar. Cover them with 2 cups of boiling water, and let them steep overnight. Strain it the next day, and you have a bottle of pale golden, delicately perfumed elderflower water. The time to gather elderflowers is June and July, but if none are available, use the dried flowers (obtainable from any good herbalist), and follow the same procedure. But with the dried flowers only use 2 tablespoons. This elderflower water can be used by itself or made into more elaborate tonics. Here are four versions, so make one up to suit yourself.

old Scottish elderflower water Put all these ingredients together into a bottle, shake and use.

3 tablespoons elderflower water
3 tablespoons rosewater
3 tablespoons witch-hazel
1 teaspoon boric acid

elderflowers and myrrh To half a cup of elderflower water slowly add four tablespoons of tincture of benzoin mixing all the time. Then add 6 drops of tincture of myrrh. Let it stand for a day, then filter. This tonic smells gorgeous, and can be equally well used as an after-shave lotion.

tonic for open pores Mix the ingredients together in a large bottle. After twelve hours filter through filter paper to get rid of the film that will have formed on the top. This simple recipe is well worth making for its lovely fresh tangy effect on the skin.

10 tablespoons elderflower water
5 tablespoons cucumber juice (see p. 40)
4 tablespoons eau de cologne
1 tablespoon tincture of benzoin

elderflowers with milk and honey Heat the milk and elderflowers together slowly, and keep on a very low heat for about 30 minutes. Remove from the heat, and let stand for three hours, after which reheat and strain. Now add the honey. Use this to cleanse your face and soften the skin. Store it in the refrigerator and use while still fresh.

½ cup buttermilk, whey or plain milk
6 tablespoons elderflowers
1 tablespoon honey

Even the leaves of the elder can be used as a skin tonic; they are considered a potent remedy for an itchy skin.

The herbs that are particularly good as skin tonics are: *Yarrow*, for greasy skin; *Camomile* is healing and astringent, and helps eliminate wrinkles; *Rosemary* is healing and firming; *Parsley* contains Vitamin C which makes it effective on spotty, patchy skins; *Tansy* lotion helps get rid of freckles; *Mint* is stimulating; *Comfrey* is healing and especially good at clearing up spotty skins; and *Fennel* makes a mild tonic which can be used as an eye lotion and as a general tonic (it is also thought to improve the memory!).

These waters normally last about a week, but will keep longer if kept in the refrigerator, although, as I have said before, the idea is to use fresh products so make small batches and use them quickly.

vinegar tonics Vinegar makes an ideal skin tonic. The skin has an acid mantle, and vinegar, being acidic, restores this. Always use the vinegar diluted one part to eight parts of water, and keep a large bottle in your bathroom to be used constantly. Use it as your final hair rinse, wash in it, or even add it to your bath water; it prevents itchiness of the skin and gets rid of that tight feeling the skin sometimes has after washing.

More aromatic vinegars are made by simply adding herbs, flowers or essential oils to the diluted vinegar. It is related, that, during the Plague of Marseilles, four robbers invented an aromatic vinegar. They claimed that it was through wearing it they were able to rob the dead and dying without fear of infection. In fact in France vinegar toilet water was long known under the name 'Vinaigre des quatre voleurs'; and the following is said to be one and the same recipe!

½ cup wine or cider vinegar
½ teaspoon cloves
1 tablespoon lavender
1 tablespoon rose petals
1 tablespoon rosemary

Rosewater or orange-flower water

Mix the vinegar, herbs and flowers together in a bottle and shake well. Leave them to stand for at least a week, shaking the bottle daily, then strain. If a stronger scent is required, repeat the whole process. Dilute with the orange-flower water or rosewater, in the proportions 8 parts water to 1 part vinegar.

cucumber tonic Cucumbers are well known for their soothing and cooling properties; any tonic containing cucumber always seems to keep very cold and that, of course, makes it most refreshing. The only trouble is that they tend to go bad rather quickly, so store them in the refrigerator and use them as soon as possible.

There are a number of ways of making cucumber skin lotions. The easiest method is to simply cut half a cucumber into chunks and put it into the liquidizer. Strain it and you have a deliciously fresh and cool cucumber lotion.

Another recipe, that lasts longer. Wash and liquidize half an unpeeled cucumber. Put this in a saucepan, bring it to the boil, and simmer it for five minutes. Cool and strain it, then add 1 tablespoon of witch-hazel to every 2 tablespoons of the cooked cucumber juice. This version does not go bad nearly as fast as the first, but it is still wise to store it in the refrigerator.

cucumber and mint stimulating tonic I think this is a heavenly combination for a summer cosmetic: it is cool, fresh and tingly, and being green, even *looks* refreshing.

½ cucumber
4 tablespoons mint

Optional: Vodka or witch-hazel and green colouring

Put the cucumber and mint into a liquidizer, and blend until the mint is very finely chopped, and then strain. If you do not have a liquidizer, then finely chop them both, and push them through a sieve (more work but the same result). After straining I add a drop of green colouring, and anything from a tablespoon to a wine-glass of vodka or witch-hazel to make it more cooling, and to make it last longer. This gives you a large bottle of beautiful fresh skin tonic, as good as, or better, than any product you could buy.

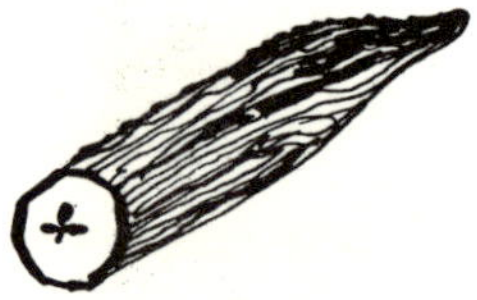

And what could be simpler?

Do not throw away the pulp left in the sieve; turn to p. 44 and use it in a mask.

oranges and lemons Put about ½ a sliced orange, a ¼ lemon and a tablespoon of castor sugar into a pan with a cup of milk. Heat this mixture to near boiling point. When cool, sieve, and it is ready for use. Keep it in the fridge. This is an unusual refreshing skin tonic suitable for all skin types.

apple tree bark tonic In Kashmir they use the bark from apple trees to make a skin tonic. Infuse 4 tablespoons of apple tree bark in 2 cups of boiling water. Add sufficient sage to give it a pleasant aroma – about 1 tablespoon. Apply this to the face and neck to rid the face of wrinkles.

Astringents

Strong skin tonics and astringents contain alcohol, but in England it is impossible to buy pure cosmetic alcohol unless one has a licence. So we have to use the nearest equivalent, which is vodka – fine for our skin, but not so good for the pocket. Otherwise we could use surgical spirit, but this smells revolting, and is extremely harsh; or witch-hazel which is good, but not as strong, and so doesn't preserve the fruit juice, or absorb the perfumes very well. So, although vodka is expensive, I think it is worth using it; we only need small amounts of it in any cosmetic and when compared with bought products, our home-made ones are still very cheap. I have never personally been in favour of astringents that are too strong, as I feel they *over*-dry the skin, leaving it feeling tight, paper-like, and dehydrated. It's far better to use a milder tonic more frequently.

honey water (or King James' skin freshener) 'The water of the honey combe' was recommended by Theophrastus, who died in 286 BC 'for preventing hair falling off and causing it to grow and cleaning the skin'. Our modern recipes for it are based on the formula devised by George Wilson, apothecary to James II. He records that, 'This water I have often made for King James II. It is an antiparlytick, smooths the skin and gives one of the most agreeable smells that can be smelt.' He also added that '40 to 50 drops added to a pint of water are enough to wash the hands and face with.' I am giving two recipes for this lotion, the first one of which is very similar to the original recipe.

2 tablespoons honey
2 teaspoons coriander seeds
2 teaspoons nutmeg
1 teaspoon cloves
4 teaspoons grated lemon peel
8 tablespoons alcohol (vodka)
4 tablespoons rosewater
4 tablespoons orange-flower water
½ teaspoon benzoin
½ teaspoon storax

Mix all the ingredients together in a large glass jar with a tightly-fitting lid. Put on the lid, and shake all the ingredients together. Let it stand for a week, shaking it vigorously every time you remember, and then filter and bottle. You will have approximately 1¼ cups of fragrant astringent lotion.

8 tablespoons alcohol (vodka)
pinch of musk grains
8 sandalwood chips or ¼ teaspoon sandalwood oil

1 teaspoon bergamot oil
¼ teaspoon lavender oil
⅛ teaspoon clove oil
4 tablespoons rosewater
4 tablespoons orange-flower water
1 tablespoon honey

musk and honey water Marinate the musk and sandalwood in the alcohol for a week, then add the rest of the ingredients. Mix them in a large bottle, cap it well and shake. Let it stand for *at least* a fortnight, shaking occasionally, then filter. This takes a while to mature so wait the whole fortnight, as it can smell quite disgusting before then. It blends beautifully in the end, however, and is well worth waiting for.

At first, the ingredients *will* seem very expensive, but once you have used the lotion, you will realize how good it is. If you cannot get sandalwood chips – they are available from Baldwins (see p.18 for address) and are very cheap – use sandalwood oil, but this is much more expensive.

This recipe is the one I always follow – a bit more expensive than the plain honey water, perhaps, but so exotic and refreshing. It is even spicy enough for a man to use, and makes a good after-shave lotion. It is quite strong, and so I make a large bottle but then fill another bottle with purified water to which I add several tablespoons of this musk and honey water. Better to dilute it at the end like this, because in this way the oils blend together more effectively.

2 tablespoons rosemary
The peel and pith of ¼ an orange and ½ a lemon
4 sprigs of mint
¼ cup alcohol (or witch-hazel)
½ cup rosewater

Hungary water There is a tradition, dating from 1235, that the original recipe for this water was given to Queen Elizabeth of Hungary by a hermit. Through using it she became so beautiful that at the age of seventy-two her hand was asked in marriage by the King of Poland. (The recipe is also considered very refreshing to the brain!)

Mix all the ingredients together in a large bottle and let them stand for at least forty-eight hours – longer if possible – shaking frequently. Then strain and bottle. If you find it too astringent, cut down the alcohol, and use witch-hazel in its place.

Rosemary, which is the principal ingredient, has a marvellous reputation, and I read that it 'ensures beauty and makes age a mere flight of time'. No wonder Hungary water has remained so popular.

lemon and peppermint astringent tonic Mix all these ingredients together in a large bottle. If you have no lemons handy, you can use bought pure lemon juice, but it is not quite as good; the fresher the better. Let it stand for a day, then strain, bottle and use. This makes about half a pint of lovely cool fresh astringent – all that menthol in the peppermint extract leaves the skin feeling sparklingly fresh. This is suitable for greasy skin as it is rather drying.

Juice of 2 large lemons (4 tablespoons)
½ teaspoon peppermint extract
8 tablespoons witch-hazel
2 tablespoons alcohol (vodka)

blue camphor tonic Mix all the ingredients together in a large bottle. Camphor tightens and tones the skin, and is especially good if you suffer from large pores and spots. Vary the amount of camphor you use to suit your skin. Sometimes I soak large squares of cotton wool in this tonic, and use it as a quick face-mask to liven up a jaded-looking skin.

½ cup rosewater
½ cup witch-hazel
½ cup distilled water
1 tablespoon camphor spirit

2 drops blue colouring

a stronger version Half a cup of the above mixed with a pinch of alum will make it even more zingy and tightening (which makes it a great after-shave). In fact alum added to any of the skin tonic recipes will make them more astringent.

pomegranate lotion Village beauties in the district of Shaghnan, N.E. Afghanistan, where women are renowned for their beauty, use pomegranate juice. They make this by boiling the peel of the fruit and then using the water as an astringent lotion. They also apply this juice to their breasts and fat areas to firm them up.

Toning masks
Masks are a marvellous way to tone and stimulate the skin, and the recipes following are designed to do just that, and will leave your skin feeling refreshed, sparklingly clean, and smooth.

egg white mask Probably the best known, most used, toning and tightening mask is the egg white. Simply spread a thin film of egg white on your face. You can use it as it is or beat it up and make it frothy. There is no difference and it's only a question of preference. Rinse off after ten to twenty minutes. This mask really tightens up the skin, ironing out wrinkles (temporarily, I'm afraid), and leaving the skin feeling smooth and satiny. It has an astringent action and so is ideal for greasy skin. If your skin is dry, add a teaspoon of oil and/or one of honey, or better still, turn to the nourishing masks section and use an egg yolk mask.

As an instant pick-me-up, or before-party treatment, this mask is unbeatable.

cucumber and yoghourt Cucumber has always been used to refine and tone the skin. Reference to its use can be found in all the old beauty books and nowadays many modern cosmetics claim it as a vital ingredient.

¼ cucumber
2 tablespoons yoghourt

Finely mash and sieve the cucumber (a liquidizer is useful here) and mix it with two tablespoons of yoghourt. This has a fairly mild astringent quality. For something stronger try this one:

Juice of ¼ cucumber
1 egg white
1 teaspoon lemon juice
1 teaspoon vodka (optional)

Mash and liquidize the cucumber, then strain the mixture to give you the juice. Beat up the egg white and slowly add the lemon juice, cucumber juice and, if your skin is greasy, the vodka.

To either of these recipes you could add a few drops of tincture of benzoin to increase the tightening qualities of the masks.

cucumber and mint Now you can be glad that you did not throw away the remains of the cucumber and mint skin tonic I gave you earlier. Use them as a mask. Depending on your skin type, or your mood, mix it with yoghourt, soothing oatmeal for cleansing, or cream and honey to nourish, or with peppermint and alum to tone, as in the following:

2 tablespoons cucumber/mint mixture
4 drops peppermint extract
pinch of alum powder

The cucumber, with mint and peppermint make this a marvellously refreshing mask. The addition of the alum tightens the skin, so if you have dry skin leave that out; otherwise it's suitable for everyone. It is such a heavenly, fresh combination that I always keep a supply in the refrigerator throughout the summer.

peppermint green mask Very tingly and drying, this mask is only suitable for greasy, oily skin.

¼ teaspoon peppermint extract or oil
1 egg white
1 teaspoon kaolin
drop of green colouring

Mix the egg white and kaolin together into a paste and add the peppermint extract and colouring. If the mixture feels too stiff for your liking, just add enough water to bring it to the consistency you like. The hot-cold effect of the peppermint makes you feel as though it really is doing you good – and it *does* tighten and stimulate the skin.

parsley and spinach tonic mask Finely chop the parsley and spinach and boil them in a cup of water for five minutes. Let this mixture cool to extract the juices fully and then strain. Use the juice either as a skin tonic or thicken it with oatmeal, yoghourt or egg white depending on your skin type.

2 tablespoons parsley
2 tablespoons spinach or cabbage

Parsley cuts down the oiliness of the skin and spinach juice contains iron. Any vegetable or herb juice can be used in this way.

camomile mask This has always been used to clear the skin and it was once used a great deal in hot poultices. Infuse a handful of dried camomile, strain after 20 minutes and use it mixed with honey and oatmeal for a lovely refreshing mask.

narcissus bulbs The women of ancient Greece soaked bread-crumbs in milk and honey or the juice from narcissus bulbs. These were spread on linen, the poultice was applied to the face and kept on overnight.

tomato toner Tomatoes are particularly useful when treating blackheads and greasy skin. The acid in the tomato thoroughly cleans the skin, thus keeping it free from clogged pores and hence discouraging blackheads.

Mash a tomato and strain through a sieve. Mix the pulp with some oatmeal and you have a lovely salmon-coloured and light toning mask. Tomato juice can also be mixed with any of the other common ingredients I mention throughout the mask section; it is especially good, for instance, with honey or yoghourt. Or simply cut a slice of tomato and rub it over the areas where you tend to get blackheads. A Spanish diplomat's wife told me that the word tomato is derived from the Spanish and was also known as 'love apple' – as it still is in parts of South America. What fun to clean one's face with a love apple.

pear peeler Pears contain a disinfectant and have an astringent action on the skin, making them especially suitable for use on greasy spotty skins. Mash one ripe pear, sieve it, and use it as it is or mix it into a paste with powdered milk. This thoroughly cleans and tones the skin, leaving it rejuvenated.

dandelion mask Dandelions are full of vitamins and are reputed to cure sallowness. If your skin is looking slightly grey try this simple mask. Mash and strain two tablespoons of stewed dandelion leaves. Apply this purée to your skin and leave it on for about fifteen minutes. Rinse off with cool water and you will find your skin glowing with health.

2 tablespoons Fullers' Earth
2 tablespoons whey
1 teaspoon orange-flower water
pinch ground cloves
pinch bicarbonate of soda
1 teaspoon honey

Turkish bleaching mask Mix all these ingredients together into a fine paste. If you have no whey use ordinary milk, but the whey is better for bleaching; it is greatly used all over the middle East, especially on discoloured necks. This mask tightens the skin, slightly bleaches it, and leaves it feeling smooth and fresh.

2 tablespoons household starch
1 tablespoon warm milk

a quickie mask Mix these together into a paste. It dries very quickly so remove after ten minutes. Your skin will feel firm and smooth.

Moisturizing and nourishing

Your skin doesn't only need cleaning, it also needs moisturizing and feeding. A moisturizer is a cream containing water which gives moisture to the skin cells, helping them to stay 'plumped-out'. A dermatologist in America discovered the necessity of moisturizers when he took callouses from the feet and soaked them in oil. Nothing happened, the callouses remaining hard and brittle, so he tried the experiment again, this time soaking them in plain water. The callouses became soft and pliable. So oil without the aid of water is not enough. The oils and waxes in the creams prevent unwanted water evaporation, and polish and lubricate the surface of the skin, but it is the combination of the oils, waxes and water that will keep your skin smooth, soft and flexible. It also protects the skin because a moisturizer acts as a barrier between your skin and the elements, and your skin and make-up.

I think moisturizers are essential for all skin types, for even greasy skin sometimes needs moisture.

The term 'nourishing cream' is really a misnomer, as nothing will actually nourish the skin. But nourishing creams will *lubricate* the skin, as they are usually thicker and richer in oils than moisturizers, making them especially good for dry and older skins. They are usually used at night simply because one has more time then, and not many people want to go about with a greasy face during the day. Nourishing cream should be well massaged into the skin, or put on before a bath (the steam helps its absorption). After about ten or twenty minutes, if there is still a film of grease on the skin, wipe it off (your skin will have absorbed all it can, and to leave excess grease on the skin only attracts the dirt and clogs the pores). So simply massage it in, then wipe off the excess.

Any skin will benefit from being cared for with creams. Leather shoes that have been cleaned and polished look better and last longer than shoes that have been neglected – and so it is with your skin (which, after all, is a surface of very fine leather).

Creams

simple moisturizer Put the waxes into a bowl and melt over the water bath. When melted add in the oil. In a separate bowl, heat the water over the same water bath so that the two bowls are at the same temperature. Slowly add the water to the melted waxes and oils, stirring all the time. Remove from heat and stir, either with a wooden spoon, or an electric mixer on low, until it sets. When cool add the lavender oil.

2 teaspoons beeswax
1 teaspoon emulsifying wax
5 teaspoons almond oil

4 tablespoons water

a few drops of lavender oil

herb cream base I make a large batch of this cream and store it in the refrigerator as the base for herb creams.

Melt the oils and waxes together over a water bath, cool and store. This recipe contains no water, so that you can use it as a base for a herb lotion. Simply take a couple of tablespoons of the basic cream, melt it and add a tablespoon of any herb (or fruit) lotion or infusion. In this way it only takes a moment to make a batch of herb cream using the herb you feel your skin needs at that moment, or one you just feel like experimenting with. This method is ideal as any cream containing fresh herb or fruit juice does tend to go bad and in this way you can easily make a small fresh batch each time you need it.

4 tablespoons lanolin
2 tablespoons white emulsifying wax
6 tablespoons beeswax
6 tablespoons almond oil

comfrey cream I frequently use the basic recipe above to make comfrey cream. Comfrey is a healing herb which is ideal if your skin is sensitive or has any irritations or spots. All the comfrey plant can be used, leaves and the root. Comfrey's major component is allantoin which is said to promote tissue building and the cell restorative action, and is renowned for its healing and softening effect on the skin.

Take a handful of comfrey, liquidize it and then strain it. The juice can be applied as it is, as a skin tonic; or better still added to our basic recipe, and you have a pot of beneficial comfrey cream.

By now you should know not to throw away the residue in the strainer; add a teaspoon of honey to a tablespoon of residue and use it as a face mask.

3 teaspoons beeswax
3 teaspoons emulsifying wax
½ cup almond oil
¼ cup avocado oil

3 tablespoons rosewater

avocado and almond cream Melt the waxes in an enamel pan over a water bath, then add the avocado and almond oils. Now add the heated rosewater drop by drop, stirring constantly. Remove from the heat, and stir intermittently while it cools. At this stage, perfume with your favourite scent – a few drops is all you need.

This recipe is foolproof, quick and easy: it takes me only about fifteen minutes to make. It also makes a very good all-purpose cream, as both almond and avocado oils are fine and rich (in fact, I have read that avocado oil is the vegetable oil most similar to our own body oil). These oils are expensive (if you can't get avocado oil, substitute sunflower or sesame) but, when you think of the cost of bought face creams, your one large cupful of lovely soft, fine cream seems cheap in comparison

4 teaspoons lanolin
2 teaspoons emulsifying wax
2 teaspoons beeswax
5 tablespoons sunflower oil

6 tablespoons water
2 teaspoons glycerine
½ teaspoon borax

sunshine sunflower moisture cream Melt the oils and waters separately over a water bath, making sure the borax is completely dissolved. While still on the heat, slowly add the waters to the oils, stir well. After a couple of minutes remove from the heat and beat, using a wooden spoon or the lowest speed of a blender. The cream will slowly whiten and become beautifully thick and creamy-textured, making about a cup of beautiful rich cream. This cream goes into the skin immediately, leaving it looking moist and soft.

2 tablespoons emulsifying wax
2 tablespoons almond or sunflower oil
1 teaspoon lanolin

½ teaspoon borax
1 teaspoon witch-hazel
1½ teaspoons glycerine
8 tablespoons water

Perfume: jasmine oil

jasmine non-greasy moisture cream These quantities give you about ¾ cup of soft white cream which is absorbed instantly and is suitable for normal and greasy skins. Melt the waxes together over a water bath, and in a separate bowl heat the borax, water and glycerine, then add the witch-hazel. Take off the heat, slowly add the waters to the oils, stir well until cool, and then add a few drops of jasmine oil. As this cream is non-greasy, it makes an excellent cream for men.

2 tablespoons cocoa butter
2 tablespoons emulsifying wax
1 tablespoon beeswax
4 tablespoons sesame oil
1 tablespoon almond oil

cocoa butter nourishing cream Heat all the ingredients together over a water bath, stirring them thoroughly. When they are completely melted, remove from the heat and stir intermittently until the cream cools. Perfume and pour into jars. These quantities make about half a cup.

If you do not have sesame or almond oil you can always substitute sunflower or safflower oil (still lovely but not quite as rich). Cocoa butter, too, is a luxurious ingredient, a soft emollient wax which is rich in polyunsaturates (as, indeed are sesame and almond oils). The final result is a firm cream which, because of its low melting point, liquifies on contact with the skin. The oils used are all expensive, and it is unlikely that cosmetic manufacturers would use them in such quantity. But *you* can, and then you will find out that you have a really superb cream which leaves the skin feeling beautifully smooth without being greasy.

a second cocoa butter cream Melt these together over a water bath, remove from the heat and mix thoroughly. These quantities make just under a cupful of thick, rich cream. It is especially good for really neglected areas and dry skin, and is marvellous to massage with. Use it on your neck, your elbows, knees, feet, anywhere that could do with some extra nourishing. If you find it too oily, simply add 2 tablespoons of water when you are letting it cool (and now you also have a rich moisturizing cream).

2 tablespoons cocoa butter
2 tablespoons lanolin
8 tablespoons almond, sesame or safflower oil

Optional: perfume

elderflower cream Put the waxes and elderflowers together in a bowl over a water bath as usual, and let them simmer together for an hour. Strain, and then add the warm water.

Another way of making elderflower cream is to use one of the recipes for a moisturizer or cleansing cream, and use elderflower water instead of plain water.

3 tablespoons almond oil
1 tablespoon lanolin
4 tablespoons elderflower blossoms

3 tablespoons water

wheatgerm nourishing cream Melt the waxes and heat the waters in the usual way (making sure you have completely dissolved the borax, for otherwise your cream will be gritty). Remove from the heat and slowly add the waters to the oils. Beat on low speed or stir until the cream is thick and glossy, making about one cup. All that lanolin and wheatgerm – which contains Vitamin E – makes this a really amazingly good nourishing cream.

1 teaspoon beeswax
1 teaspoon emulsifying wax
5 tablespoons lanolin
3 tablespoons sesame oil
2 tablespoons wheatgerm oil

5 tablespoons water
1 tablespoon witch-hazel
½ teaspoon borax

perfume

extra rich vitamin cream Vitamin E seems to be very popular as a healer, and although at first I was very sceptical (there is no medical proof of its effectiveness) so many people swear by it that there must be something to it. I am constantly being told that it has healed scar tissue, improved spotty skin, eased out lines, and restored elasticity to the skin. Vitamin E oil is rather thick and sticky and can, of course, be used by itself, but I find it much better made into a cream. (There are Vitamin E tablets which can be taken internally and are said to increase the circulation.)

The other vitamin popular in skin-care is Vitamin A. It counteracts dry, scaly skin and irritations, and is reputed to protect against infections and to heal wounds. Carrot oil is a great source of Vitamin A, and I have read that carotene acts on the lymphatic system, causing the disappearance of wrinkles and bags under the eyes. It is a very fine thin oil which goes in immediately, making it ideal for use in eye creams.

So here is one of my favourite recipes using vast amounts of both these vitamins.

1 tablespoon beeswax
1 tablespoon emulsifying wax
1 tablespoon lanolin
3 tablespoons wheatgerm oil (Vit. E)
3 tablespoons carrot oil (Vit. A)

6 tablespoons distilled water
½ teaspoon borax
2 drops tincture of benzoin

Perfume: orange-flower oil

Melt the waxes and oils over a water bath, and at the same time in a separate bowl, dissolve the borax in the warm water. Quickly add the water to the oils, and beat until it cools slightly. Then add the tincture of benzoin, and carry on beating until the cream sets. You will have made nearly a cup of firm, orange cream.

If you cannot get hold of either wheatgerm or carrot oil, don't worry, but use five tablespoons of almond oil and put in 4 to 6 capsules of both Vitamins E and A. (Simply prick open the capsules and add the contents at the same time as the benzoin.)

This is one of the richest, finest creams imaginable, and with these massive doses of vitamin oils, it really nourishes your skin. I always use it after I have been in the sun when my skin needs all the feeding it can get.

rejuvenating honey cream When I asked for recipes and hints from several friends who make their own cosmetics, I kept getting the same answer – *HONEY*. It is quite amazing how honey can be used for everything. It is renowned for being a natural healer; it attracts and holds moisture to the skin – ideal for counteracting dryness; and repairs and softens coarse and sensitive skin. In fact, whatever your skin type, honey can help, so use it in face masks, skin tonics, face creams, and even hair conditioners.

The only trouble with honey is that it is so sticky, but this next recipe avoids that. If you don't feel like making a whole pot of cream, simply add a small amount of this one to a pot you have already made or, if by now you have a favourite recipe, add a teaspoon of honey to it.

Melt the oils together and slowly add the water, beating fairly fast and continuously for the first minute, and then more slowly, until it cools. This is a healing cream, and I add the lecithin for extra nourishment. These quantities make about a cup of pale creamy-coloured, firm cream or, if you leave out the water, you have about half a cup of clear, rather greasy cream. Both versions are marvellous, although I prefer it with water, and use the cream lavishly. When you first apply it, it feels a little tacky, but it soaks in almost immediately. It is also particularly good for sallow skins as honey can bring a glow of colour to the skin, so use it daily.

This is one of the creams you *don't* need to refrigerate; in too cold a temperature it tends to separate.

3 tablespoons lanolin
½ tablespoon honey
1 teaspoon lecithin

4 tablespoons warm water

Perfume

mixed vegetable cream Melt the waxes and oils together over a water bath, and in a separate pan dissolve the borax in the water. Add the water to the oils, and remove from the heat and beat (low speed on a mixer) until the cream cools. Add the perfume, and there you are with 1½ cups of thick, penetrating, glossy cream, which leaves no sign of grease but gives the skin a satiny sheen.

I used all these different oils to make the cream really nourishing, but if you prefer you can simply use 7 tablespoons almond and 7 tablespoons sesame or even 14 of one oil (but that is a bit unimaginative and you should experiment). By using a combination of oils you are getting the best from them all.

I perfume this with amber oil which has an unusual smell, I feel, particularly suited to all these vegetable oils.

2 tablespoons beeswax
4 tablespoons emulsifying wax
3 teaspoons lanolin
4 tablespoons almond oil
4 tablespoons sesame oil
2 tablespoons avocado oil
2 tablespoons safflower oil
2 tablespoons sunflower oil

5 tablespoons water
½ teaspoon borax

Perfume: amber oil

scrumptious strawberry cream Strawberries are in season for so short a time that we must make the most of them while we can. I buy the damaged ones at the end of the day and make a strawberry jam lotion which I then keep in the refrigerator and use in face masks, creams and lotions through the year.

Put the strawberries and sugar in a pan and bring to the boil, cool and bring to the boil again, bottle and keep in the refrigerator. This 'jam' can then be kept and used in any recipe calling for strawberry juice. This juice is obtained by sieving either fresh or 'jam' strawberries. If you use fresh add half a teaspoon of sugar. Strawberries are acid and are rich in vitamins and enzymes, and so reduce oiliness, help circulation and thoroughly cleanse the skin.

1 kilo, 800g (4 lbs) strawberries
450g (1 lb) sugar

Melt the wax and add all the other ingredients. Remove from the heat and stir by hand until it becomes cool. This cream is a lovely soft, pale pink, smells heavenly and feels incredibly luxurious. These quantities make about half a cup.

2 tablespoons strawberry juice
2 teaspoons emulsifying wax
4 teaspoons mucilage of tragacanth
2 teaspoons almond oil
1 teaspoon witch-hazel

You might have difficulty in obtaining mucilage of tragacanth, but an obliging chemist should be able to get it for you. But if even he fails you, use the strawberry juice mixed in with the basic recipe I give for a herb cream (see p. 47).

2 teaspoons lanolin
2 teaspoons emulsifying wax
2 teaspoons sunflower oil

2 tablespoons strawberry juice
3 drops benzoin

another strawberry cream Melt the waxes and oils together and then add the strawberry juice and benzoin. Remove from the heat and stir until it sets. You now have half a cup of scrumptious strawberry cream.

2 tablespoons lanolin
2 tablespoons sunflower oil

2 tablespoons strawberry juice

another simple version Melt the lanolin and oil together, and add the strawberry juice. Remove from the heat and stir thoroughly.

3 tablespoons coconut oil
2 tablespoons olive oil
1 tablespoon almond oil
½ tablespoon beeswax

3½ tablespoons water
½ teaspoon borax

Perfume

South Sea Island cream Melt the oils and waxes together over a water bath in the usual way, remove from the heat and slowly add the heated water, in which you have dissolved the borax. Stir until cool, and it will gradually become a pure white, soft cream. In the South Seas and all over South America and India, coconut oil is very widely used. It has a low melting point and so although hard it melts on touching the skin or when in the sun, which gives this cream a very fine consistency. These proportions will give you about three-quarters of a cup of delicious cream, which I perfume with an exotic 'hot climate' flower scent like jasmine or frangipani.

2 teaspoons beeswax
2 teaspoons emulsifying wax
8 teaspoons almond oil
4 teaspoons lanolin
4 teaspoons coconut oil

6 teaspoons orange-flower water
3 drops tincture of benzoin

Perfume: orange oil

orange-flower skin food Melt the waxes and oils together and add the heated orange-flower water and benzoin, stirring all the time. Beat until you have about half a cup of beautiful white cream which is absorbed instantly into the skin and constant use of which should help to obliterate lines and wrinkles. Perfume it with orange oil.

2 tablespoons lanolin
2 tablespoons almond oil
1 tablespoon apricot oil

3 teaspoons lemon juice

Perfume

apricot anti-wrinkle cream Melt the lanolin and oils together and then add in the lemon juice and perfume. Apricots are rich in Vitamin A and the oil is very fine and nourishing. When the cream is cool give it a final whip-up, and you will have about three-quarters of a cup of elegant, creamy, rich, anti-wrinkle cream.

Afghan nourishing face cream 'Cook the top of the milk, skim off the skin into a little muslin bag and rub your face with it' (*Junaid Aga*).

Nourishing masks

One thing to remember about all these delicious masks is that they needn't only be used on your face: how about giving those neglected feet, elbows and knees a treat as well!

nourishing egg yolk mask When looking through beauty recipes, time and again I come across references to the miraculous properties of the egg. The yolk is full of lecithin and protein, and is very nourishing.

1 egg yolk
1 teaspoon almond oil

Mix together, apply and leave on the face for ten to thirty minutes. (A beautiful Belgian countess uses this every other day, and is convinced that is why her skin has remained youthful and soft.) Cream can also be added to make it even more nutritious, and you could use the whole egg instead of just the yolk. Experiment to find out what most benefits your skin.

1 whole egg
1 teaspoon honey
1 teaspoon almond oil

lemon egg mask Use half a squeezed lemon as a bowl and put the yolk of an egg in it. Add a couple of drops of lemon juice and allow the mixture to stand for about half an hour. The oils from the lemon soak into the egg yolk and make this mask ideal for greasy skins.

lecithin mask Powdered lecithin is very nutritious being a complex substance containing phosphorous and protein, and is found in eggs and soya beans.

1 tablespoon lecithin
2 teaspoons peach or any fruit juice
1 teaspoon wheatgerm oil

Mix together and smooth on to the face. This is one of my favourite masks, rich, nourishing and pampering.

egg and yeast mask Mix these together into a smooth paste and apply. Leave it on for about fifteen minutes and rinse off with milk. The yeast stimulates the skin, and with the addition of the egg yolk and oil, is a most effective mask.

1 egg yolk
1 tablespoon brewers' yeast
1 teaspoon sunflower oil

a Hungarian country mask Stir all these ingredients into a paste and apply as a nourishing mask. It can also be used as skin food, and left on the face. The recipe was given to me by a Hungarian woman whose whole family use it, and we all know how beautiful Hungarian women are.

2 tablespoons very well-cooked rice
1 tablespoon almond oil
1 egg yolk
1 teaspoon honey
6 drops lemon juice

avocado mask The avocado is one of the most nutritious fruits: it contains a great number of vitamins, minerals and natural oils which can all help feed the skin.

2 tablespoons ripe avocado pear
1 teaspoon liquid honey
Couple of drops lemon juice

Mash and sieve the avocado with a couple of drops of lemon juice to prevent it going black. Add the honey and mix together into a paste; apply, and leave on for as long as you can. In South Africa this recipe is used to counteract the drying effect of the sun. It is a delicious mask, softening, moisturizing and nourishing the skin. A girl from California even uses this mask on her hair!

mayonnaise Crazy as it sounds, mayonnaise is an amazing beauty aid for all skin types. It has everything we need, oil to lubricate, eggs to nourish, and vinegar to retain the acid mantle. An American model I know uses it everywhere: her face, her hair, her body, and is convinced that it has done miracles for her skin.

2 egg yolks
2 tablespoons vinegar (cider vinegar preferably)
¾ cup olive oil

This mayonnaise can be used as a basis for masses of different fruit masks: avocadoes, strawberries, tomatoes, cucumbers, in fact anything you have around. If you don't have time to make your own mayonnaise, use a ready-made one, and an added egg yolk will make it almost as good as the home-made version.

½ apple, peeled and sliced
1 tablespoon honey
1 teaspoon ascorbic acid
1 egg yolk
1 tablespoon cider vinegar
3 tablespoons oil
(or 2 tablespoons of your mayonnaise)

apple mask Put all these ingredients into a liquidizer and blend until completely smooth. This is a most effective mask for all skin types: the vinegar restores the acid mantle; the apples contain pectin which is soothing; the ascorbic acid, Vitamin C, prevents the apple turning brown, and the honey, egg, and oil are all highly nutritious. So, in one mask, we have a complete beauty treatment.

In a book written in 1808 I found this recipe: 'A preservative for the face: Apply slices of veal cutlets after which you apply the waters of green apples.' I feel we can omit the first stage, but by using our apple recipe, we are following instructions and applying apple water! Emma, Lady Hamilton, is said to have always washed in water in which apples had been boiled. Even the idea of applying meats to the face is quite often referred to. The Empress Elizabeth of Austria and the ladies of the Court of Louis XIV were all said to have used raw meat masks. I have tried most things, but this is one I think I can do without!

face pack The Phoenicians, long skilled in the arts of beauty culture, concocted a fig and thyme face pack, to render ladies' faces smooth and soft after a day in the hot sun. The figs were boiled until soft, in honey water, and added to a mixture of dried thyme leaves, pounded in a mortar, and applied.

the food of paradise One of the really ancient recipes for a beautifying face mask is contained in a marvellous traditional story from the East. A young man sets off to seek his fortune. Resting by a river, he finds that the water is bringing down, every day, a packet of delicious nougat. He eats this and feels compelled to discover its source. Eventually he comes upon a beautiful princess who is throwing away the packets which contain a confection made of ground almonds and honey – the basis of her daily face-pack!

2 teaspoons ground almonds
1 teaspoon rosewater
½ teaspoon liquid honey

Mix these ingredients together into a paste and spread on the face. Leave for fifteen minutes. Wash off with rosewater.

cream and honey mask What could be more nutritious than thick double cream? So instead of that extra spoonful on your pudding, put it on your face.

1 tablespoon double cream
1 tablespoon honey

Mix together and apply. Leave it on as long as possible then rinse off with warm water. Your skin will be left glowing and incredibly soft. A Greek woman who has a beautiful complexion recommended a mixture of milk and honey to preserve the skin. When she is cooking she has a bowl of this mixture next to her. She ties back her hair and applies the mixture to her face, with a wooden spoon, as often as possible during the time she is in the kitchen. If her skin is anything to go by, it is most certainly worth trying.

almonds and cream Almonds are widely used in cosmetics for their nutritious properties.

1 tablespoon finely-ground almonds
1 tablespoon double cream

Mix the ground almonds into a paste with the cream. An Indian woman I know always massages her face with this mixture – thus rubbing away any dead skin cells and nourishing her skin at the same time. If you find it too abrasive to massage with (although I am in favour of that slight abrasive action), simply apply the mixture as a mask, and rinse it off with rosewater.

West Indian banana mask In the West Indies where there is an abundance of bananas, the women keep their faces wrinkle-free by using this nutritious mask.

½ ripe banana
1 teaspoon honey
2 teaspoons cream

Mash and sieve the banana, then add the honey and cream. Bananas are very rich and soothing and this mask is marvellous for a dry skin. If your skin is greasy add one teaspoon of fresh orange juice which has a slight astringent action.

One of the most interesting things about collecting recipes is the fact that the same ingredients are used all over the world. In a manuscript from Afghanistan a treatment that is recommended for convalescents is to massage them with a mixture of milk and bananas. Another recipe from the same manuscript which is especially for softening and nourishing dry skin: equal parts of cream cheese and powdered walnuts mixed with enough rosewater to make a light paste.

green pepper mask These are surprisingly nutritious. Liquidize them and use the juice, mixed with any of the masks, to make a feeding mask.

Flemish wrinkle eraser Soak geranium leaves in rosewater, and then put them whole onto your face. This is renowned for softening the skin and erasing wrinkles. Obviously to be able to do this, you have to be lying down (a nice excuse for a rest!).

Skin problems

Blackheads, spots and acne are unfortunately all too common. They are a reflection of one's health, diet, cleansing habits and emotional state.

Blackheads are caused by over-active sebaceous glands, which produce an excess of sebum. This oil comes up through the pores and if there is already grease or dirt blocking the exit a bump forms under the skin. This hardens into a plug, the top of which, when oxidized by the air, turns black, thus forming a blackhead. They used to be called 'worms in the face' and when extracted they fit this description exactly.

Sometimes this sebum festers causing a sore bump, or *spot*. If this spot becomes infected it erupts forming a pustule or pus-filled spot. This pus is infectious – so try not to allow the infection to spread by being scrupulously clean: a large number of these spots, lead to acne.

Acne is normally caused by an imbalance in the hormones, which is why so many teenagers suffer from it. Nervousness and anxiety, as we are all too well aware, are also responsible for many outbreaks of spots. The tension affects the hormonal balance, causing an increase in the perspiration and oily secretions, and we get spots.

How to cure the problems

The most vital treatment is thorough cleanliness. Keep your skin scrupulously clean, washing it at every opportunity, preferably at least three times a day.

Watch your diet. Over-eating of starchy food may cause the glands to become more active, so try to avoid fried food, sugary foods, and too much coffee or starch. Instead eat lots of fresh fruit and green vegetables, and drink plenty of water. Start the morning with a glass of hot lemon juice and throughout the day drink as much water as possible (at least eight glasses, as this clears the body of toxins thus clearing the skin). Yeast tablets are often recommended to people with spots and they help with the majority of cases. Exercises and fresh air increase the circulation bringing the blood to the skin, which helps the healing and bacteria-fighting process and improves the skin.

Never fiddle with your skin. I am very anti magnifying mirrors and over-strong lights over bathroom mirrors – they show up all those tiny imperfections that we all have and which would be best left alone. Just before going to bed when you are tired you may see these and start to fiddle. *Don't* – it is fatal. If you absolutely must do something about that blackhead, do it when you have time to give yourself a proper treatment: steam your face as I describe in the cleansing section, then, using a fresh piece of cotton wool or tissue each time, squeeze and dab with antiseptic. Forcing them out brutally can damage the under layers of the skin so be gentle. When you have finished apply a toning, skin-tightening mask.

So remember: never touch or pick at your face unless you have time to give yourself a proper facial.

If you have very bad pustular acne the heat from the steaming can spread the condition. So instead, apply a mask each day to keep the skin thoroughly clean and wait until the spots are better before steaming. Skin that is prone to acne is often very sensitive, so do not use any products that are too harsh or irritating, and whether you use creams and oils depends on your own skin.

A mark left from a spot is not usually there for life, so don't get too depressed by it. The skin is constantly renewing itself, the old cells die and flake away to be replaced by new ones, and so most scars disappear quite quickly. Dermatologists have found they can successfully treat acne with some of the new antibiotics and so if your skin is very bad I would advise you to go to your doctor or a beauty salon for professional help.

Beauty foods

As a good skin starts with what you eat, here are a couple of recipes which are most beneficial to the skin.

2 cups dark green spinach
1 cup parsley
3 cups orange juice

complexion cocktail Mix all the ingredients in a liquidizer and sieve. The mixture is quite delicious and works wonders on the complexion, as it is rich in iron and Vitamin C which are needed for a clear complexion. If you drink a couple of glasses of this cocktail each day the improvement in your skin is incredible. When watercress is in season, add a handful to the original mixture.

prune cocktail Another great beauty food to clear the skin is made from prunes. Stew a packet of prunes in the juice and peel from two lemons, then purée. Every morning drink a wine glass of this mixture. It is quite delicious and most effective in clearing the skin.

liquorice Liquorice sticks are also most beneficial to the skin, presumably because of the laxative effect.

Masks

Camphor, sulphur, yoghourt, yeast, Fuller's Earth, herbs and vegetable juices are all useful in treating bad skin. Use a mask as often as possible to cleanse the skin thoroughly – every day if you can. The following recipes, and many others in the toning and cleansing sections, are all suitable.

yoghourt A treatment for acne which is highly thought of in the Middle East is to apply a mask of plain yoghourt each day. Leave it on for ten minutes then rinse off. The enzymes in the yoghourt act on the bacteria and clean the skin. I have seen amazing results by prescribing this simple treatment.

kelp Dried seaweed, which is rich in mineral salts and iodine, is well known for its healing effect on the skin. It is widely used in Germany, and a Bavarian woman gave me this most effective recipe.

1 tablespoon kelp
1 tablespoon yoghourt

Mix into a smooth paste. Apply every other day and your skin should soon clear up and be blemish-free.

yarrow On the continent they often use hot poultices to bring a spot to a head: use comfrey, camomile, houseleek or yarrow. Yarrow is an antiseptic herb and a friend told me she always applies it to heal spots and boils; she chews yarrow leaves (fresh or dried) before putting them on cuts to stop the bleeding.

Russian comfrey This is one of the best-known herbs for healing and clearing up spots, as it is so gentle. I have already described other ways of using comfrey in the moisturizing section and these are all suitable for blemished skins. Extract the juice from 4 large comfrey leaves, either by mashing and sieving or, if you are lucky, with a juice extractor. Use this by itself or mix it into a paste with one tablespoon of kaolin. If you cannot find fresh comfrey, use the dried herb and make a strong infusion. And while you're at it, why not plant some comfrey plants to be ready for use on your next spot?

onion juice Onion juice has always been used in the treatment of skin problems and is said to prevent blemishes and wrinkles. Use the juice of an onion (it'll be hard work, mashing and sieving the onion) which you can use either by itself or mixed into a paste with kaolin or Fuller's Earth and 1 teaspoon of honey. A Belgian friend of mine who worked in the Resistance during the war told me that when they had no antiseptic they always used onion juice.

garlic Garlic also has antiseptic qualities, and this mask is one of my favourites. An Englishman living in Belgium gave me the recipe. He always used it, and also made it up for all the women in his office.

1 clove garlic
1 teaspoon kaolin
1 teaspoon honey
1 teaspoon carrot juice
1 egg white

Beat the egg white to a froth, then add the other ingredients, including the crushed clove of garlic, beating all the time. Don't be put off this mask by the slight smell, as it evaporates very quickly and the results make it well worth while.

sulphur In the island of Montserrat in the West Indies, the simple islanders know nothing about modern face masks, but since earliest times have used mud from sulphur springs for refining their skin. Wealthy women from all over the world go to Abano in Italy to have exactly the same treatment – mud baths – at tremendous cost!

sulphur mud pack Sulphur is a disinfectant and is used in the treatment of acne in many salons. Some people are allergic to it, however, so first mix up a little powdered sulphur and water and apply some behind the ear as a skin test. If there is no reaction after a couple of hours, use this mask on your face.

1 teaspoon sulphur powder
2 tablespoons Fuller's Earth
1 egg white

Use enough water to form these ingredients into a workable paste, which will depend on the size of the egg white. The Fuller's Earth is full of minerals and also has tightening and drawing properties. This mask can be used every day.

1 tablespoon raspberries
1 teaspoon yoghourt
1 teaspoon oatmeal

raspberries Mash and sieve the raspberries, then mix in the yoghourt and oatmeal until you have a smooth paste. Apply and rinse off after about twenty minutes. This mask not only smells quite beautiful but is a highly effective cleansing and treatment mask. Raspberries contain a great deal of Vitamin C and recently a doctor told me that Vitamin C was necessary for the rapid healing and growth of healthy tissue; it is said to be absorbed through the skin, so it could be of great value in the treatment of bad skin conditions. Even if you do not suffer from a bad skin, it is worth trying this mask as it really leaves the skin feeling so beautifully clean and smooth.

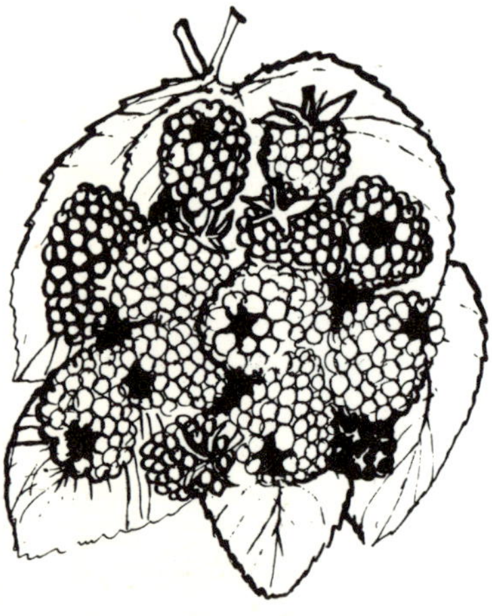

camphor BP Camphor has a healing, soothing and tightening effect on the skin and is widely used to cure spots. Be sure to use camphor BP, *not* moth balls (which contain synthetic substances harmful to the skin).

½ teaspoon camphor BP crystals
½ teaspoon oatmeal
1 teaspoon orange-flower water

Mix together and apply, and your skin will glow with health. Two to three drops of camphor spirit could be used instead of the crystals. A well-known society beautician always used to recommend her clients to add a few drops of spirit of camphor to the washing and rinsing water. This is very good for tightening and toning the skin, and diminishing those large pores. The spirit of camphor can also be used in masks (as in the one below), and you only need a couple of drops for the astringent, toning effect.

Mix together and apply, leave on for fifteen minutes, and wash off with warm water. Another stronger astringent skin tonic is also made with camphor spirit.

1 tablespoons tomato juice
1 teaspoon honey
2 drops camphor spirit

Put all these ingredients together in a large bottle and shake well. Use every day to improve your skin.

1 tablespoon glycerine
½ tablespoon powdered borax
1 cup distilled water
2-3 drops camphor spirit

a disinfectant mask After extracting blackheads, mix one tablespoon of kaolin into a paste with a few drops of 10-volume peroxide. This is a very powerful mask and should only be left on for about five minutes.

plum mask Mash the insides of 6 boiled plums and mix with a teaspoon of almond oil. This is an astringent mask especially good for acne sufferers.

Disguising your spots

If you are going out and a spot has appeared, as they always do, in a most obvious place – on your cheek, chin, or right in the middle of your forehead or cleavage – instead of covering it up with make-up, disguise it with a patch.

Patches are thought to have first been used by a court beauty who wished to do just this and hide a disfiguring spot on her cheek. It looked so becoming that she continued to use it, and they soon became fashionable, being used to cover smallpox scars. Their use became so exaggerated that one 'belle' of the 1650s had a horse and cart riding across her forehead! The fashion declined but was revived again in the reign of Queen Anne, and I feel sure that it is time for a further – though modified – revival.

The patches were made out of black velvet material, and if you

are lucky you might find a box of them in an antique shop. If not, cut circles, stars or clubs out of black velvet, or use silver stars or sequins.

'The sun and moon by her bright eyes
Eclipsed and darkened in the skies
Are but black patches that she wears
Cut into suns and moons and stars.'
Hudibras, Butler

Face massage

Once you have lines and wrinkles nothing, bar plastic surgery, can get rid of them. Massage, however, can help prevent new lines appearing (although, unfortunately, it can't vanquish the old ones there already). Why not treat yourself and your skin, and give yourself a facial using the following massage movements. Or better still, use them each time you apply all the face creams you have made. Prevention is better (and cheaper) than cure.

How does massage help? By toning up the muscles, and by nourishing both superficially with the cream and internally by bringing the blood to the surface. There are three basic movements – stroking, pinching and stimulating.

Throat and chin

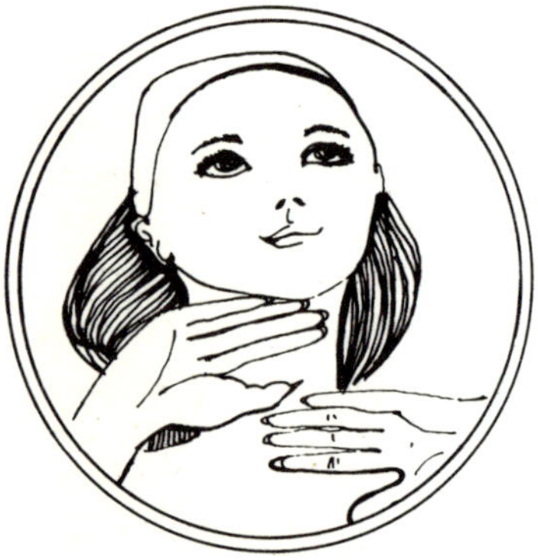

1. Start at the base of the throat, applying the cream or oil by stroking with both hands up the neck to the chin and then out to the edge of the jaw bone. I personally find it more convenient to use the back of the hand but this is up to you. The movement is a deep, swift, stroking.

2. Using the back of your hands do a swift, rolling, stroking movement, one finger after another. From the base of the neck, up and out, all the way under the chin.

3. With the thumb and fore-finger pinch the skin. Start at the edge of the jawbone and work towards the centre of the chin and back again. Repeat at least six times.

Two renowned beauties have both told me that they would never have double chins because they do this 'pinching' each day. It does not hurt and is really stimulating. Do it whenever you have a free moment – waiting for the kettle to boil, or at the traffic lights.

4. Now further stimulate by slapping your skin. This is a firm, bouncy, slapping movement. Start at the collar bone and work up the neck to the chin. It is easiest to use the front of your fingers on the neck and the back of your hand under the chin.

Cheeks

1. Apply cream using the first, second and third fingers and stroking up from the chin to the temples. Massage the corners of your mouth with a firm but gentle stroking movement. Move upwards with alternate hands, working from the chin to the nostrils.

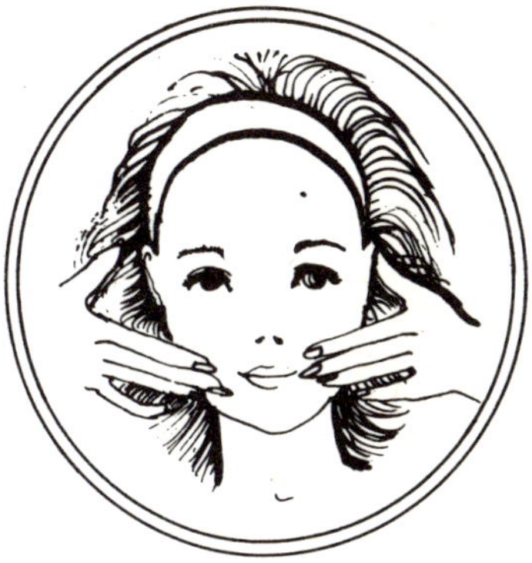

2. 'Pinch' from the corners of the mouth to the eyes.

3. Stimulate by doing small rotary movements starting at the chin and working up the nose and out across the forehead. Use the second and third fingers for this.

4. Stimulate by rolling the skin. Using the back of both hands, stroke upwards hard and fast, from jaw to cheekbone, first on one side and then the other.

Forehead

1. Using all your fingers and keeping your hands horizontal and following each other rhythmically stroke up towards the hairline.

2. Using three fingers do gentle pressures up to the hairline, working out to the temples, so that the whole forehead is covered.

3. Stroke firmly up the nose and out across the forehead to give a gentle pressure in the temples. This is also ideal for relieving tension.

4. The scissor movement. Using the fore- and middle fingers in a horizontal position work them across the forehead in a scissor movement. This helps obliterate those frown lines and I also find it great for getting rid of headaches.

5. Another marvellous way of relieving headaches is by stroking the forehead and head with the softest touch possible. Hardly touch the skin. I learnt this in Turkey and, amazing as it sounds, this faint, feathery touch really works. I have even been able to cure clients' migraines with this. So next time anyone you know has a headache try the 'fairy' touch.

Eyes

1. Pinch the eyebrows working from the nose out. Squeeze the eyebrows using the forefinger and thumb. This releases the tension that accumulates all around the eyes. Repeat several times.

2. Using the second and third fingers slowly stroke around the eyes, applying pressures at the bridge of the nose and at the temples. Always take great care not to pull or drag the skin around the eyes as it is very delicate.

To finish your massage, wipe off the residual grease, and spray with skin tonic or mineral water. Your skin will feel completely different – soft and glowing. If you have time, complete the facial treatment by giving yourself a mask (see pp. 43-46).

Cover the whole face, except the eye area where you leave the oil. Cover your eyes with cotton-wool pads soaked in eye lotion, and lie back and relax for at least fifteen to twenty minutes. Rinse off. Now look at yourself. You are rejuvenated, you feel refreshed, your eyes are bright, and your skin is as soft and smooth as a baby's.

Isometrics

Your face reflects not only your age but also your character; frowning, smiling, and laughing are all going to leave their mark on your face. This is probably why, as children, we were always being told not to pull faces as the wind would change and we would be left like that. And as you get older the muscles of the face begin to sag, making lines appear.

By doing isometrics (or face exercises), you strengthen and tighten the muscles and, as you stimulate the blood supply, they also help to nourish the skin. At least half the faces you pull are superfluous, anyway, and you need to guard particularly against habitual expressions. You won't notice these yourself so get a friend to point them out. I discovered that I was always frowning, especially when driving, so now I keep a roll of transparent adhesive in the car and stick a piece between my eyebrows. This way I feel my frown coming and can stop it. The Russian grandmother of a friend of mine taught her as a child not to pull unnecessary facial grimaces and it has paid off – she has no lines. (One often notices that men have less lines than women, and I am sure that one of the reasons for this is that they do what virtually amounts to isometric exercises every time they shave.)

In conclusion, isometrics do not actually *erase* lines but they can *diminish* them, and by doing exercises you will at least prevent them coming. So let's get exercizing!

The whole face
Try and push the face *out*. It's really an internal feeling, stretching the skin tautly over the face. Hold it like that to a count of four, relax and repeat.

Neck
Although it supports the head and is always in evidence, the neck very often gets forgotten (the face is beautifully cleaned and made-up, for example, and the poor neck is neglected). So try to nourish and look after it, as it tends to age faster than the face and it is almost impossible to disguise a lined, craggy neck.

One of the most important exercises is to hold your head up, so practice walking around with a book on your head. Then see if you can write with the book still balancing there. Afterwards, remember the position of your head when you had the book on it, and this will make you walk more gracefully, and help prevent a double chin.

These exercises will not only improve your looks and posture, but will also ease your aches and tensions. Most people, at some time or another, get an aching neck and shoulders, and this tensions leads to stiffness and headaches.

1. Stand or sit with your back straight and shoulders down and relaxed. Drop your head forward. The head weighs about six pounds; let its weight pull the head down, and feel those muscles stretch at the back of the neck. Bring your head upright again and drop it backwards. Do this exercise unhurriedly, and repeat six times.

2. Sitting in the same position drop your head to the right side, so that your ear nearly touches your shoulder. Feel the neck muscles stretch. Bring your head upright again and drop it to the left. Allow a count of two for each movement and repeat six times.

3. The same position again, but this time instead of dropping your head to the side, turn it. Try to get your chin parallel to your shoulder with each turn. Do the whole exercise four times. Then rotate your head four times to the right then four to the left. This not only uses all the neck muscles but helps get rid of a 'dowager's hump' and relieves tension from the back of the neck.

4. Slowly roll the head around, front, left, back, right, and to the front again. Do this four times going clockwise then repeat going anti-clockwise. I think this is my favourite exercise – you feel all the muscles at the back of your neck working and it leaves your

head feeling lighter and clearer (if a trifle dizzy at first).

Chin and jaw

1. Lean your head as far back as possible and open your mouth. Jutting your chin well out, slowly push it up until your mouth closes. Repeat this several times and you will feel all the muscles working.

2. Try to touch your nose with your tongue.

3. Touch the roof of your mouth with the base of your tongue (this draws up the chin).

4. Draw down the outer edges of your mouth as far as possible, hold and repeat.

5. Clasp your hands behind your head and push your resisting head into your pressing hand. Do it slowly to the count of eight. Repeat four times. Now reverse the whole exercise by pushing the head forward with a gentle firm pressure.
Needless to say, do these by yourself, or you will have the family watching you instead of TV!

Mouth and cheeks

One of the first places that lines appear is around the mouth.

1. Put the forefingers at the corners of the mouth and stretch the mouth as wide as possible. Relax and repeat. Now keeping the fingers there try and pull the mouth shut, forcing the muscles to work. Hold for a count of six, relax and repeat. That should help prevent a few of those lines.

2. Open your mouth so wide that it hurts. Close it very slowly with tension. Repeat this ten times. For the jowl, repeat this exercise but turn your head from left to right. Repeat often.

3. With your mouth open thrust your jaw out as far as possible and relax. Pull it in hard, relax, push it out to the right, relax and then to the left. This is difficult to do at first.

4. Blow out your cheeks as if you were blowing up an extremely hard balloon. Relax and repeat several times.

5. Open your mouth to form a small 'O', pull in the lips to make this as tight as possible. Now try to open your mouth, keeping the tension in your lips.

6. For those lines going from the upper lip to the nostrils. Put your thumbs under these lines and push upwards, resist with the lip muscle. Push for a count of six, relax and repeat.

7. And finally with your mouth closed give a large false smile. Relax and repeat.

Forehead and eyes

1. Without moving the rest of your face and certainly without wrinkling your forehead try to move your forehead, pushing it up and backwards towards the hairline. Practise with a mirror and you will soon find it easy. Hold the upwards pull for a count of six and relax. Do this as often as possible to counteract frowning.

2. For the eyes, open them as wide as possible, hold and relax.

3. Now slide your eyes to look at the four corners of the wall opposite, i.e. a square. Repeat going the other way.

4. Now roll your eyes around, nearly the same as the last one but this time in a circle. Do it slowly, first one way then the other.

5. Keeping the eyes closed, contract the muscles by blinking hard. Hold with the muscles taut for a few seconds. This diminishes puffiness.

6. And last for drooping eye lids. Put your middle fingers into the corners of your eyes when open. As you gently squeeze the eye shut, you can feel the muscle there working away.

If we did even a couple of these exercises each day, we would be helping to keep our faces looking young. Nowadays there are muscle-exercizing machines to help us and if they are regularly used for half an hour a day the results are fantastic. This was brought home to me by the story of an eighteen-year-old who was selling these muscle-stimulating machines, and who decided to carry out her own experiment. When she demonstrated the machines she only used the right-hand side of her face – within a fortnight, amazingly, that side was infinitely more sculptured than the other. But even without a machine we can do the preceding exercises whenever we have a spare moment – and can all benefit from them.

EYES

It does not matter what size, colour or shape your eyes are: if they are bright and sparkling they look beautiful. Eyes, more than anything else, reflect the way you feel: if you're happy, they dance and shine; equally if you're bored, tired or miserable, your eyes will instantly mirror it by looking dull and listless.

They are also affected by your general health, and by your diet. Sleep is by far the most important factor, without which, however good you feel, your eyes look bloodshot, puffy, and encircled by black shadows. Similarly, to show how much diet also affects your eyes, think of their pinkness and puffiness after you've had too much to drink. The same applies when you suffer from bilious or liverish attacks, so watch your diet. The old wives' tale that carrots make you see in the dark is not strictly true, but as carrots contain Vitamin A – very necessary for total general health – they do make your eyes glow! The same, of course, applies to all fresh vegetables.

As I have already mentioned, I am a great believer in drinking lots of water, for by clearing the body of toxins, it also clears the eyes. If you suffer from puffiness in the early morning, a glass of water first thing will help enormously. Some people recommend a glass of hot lemon juice or diluted cider vinegar for this early-morning drink, but I personally prefer plain, cold, delicious water.

Puffiness can be due to lots of things: to lack of sleep, bad diet, airless rooms, or heavy creams. The latter should never be left on overnight. If your skin is dry, *dab* on your cream, being careful not to pull the skin, then blot off the surplus. Remember that this area is so delicate that you must never apply anything that would tighten or stretch the skin; so no astringents or masks (except perhaps, a fruit mask, which would be non-drying and nourishing).

1 tablespoon lanolin
1½ tablespoons almond oil

1 teaspoon powdered lecithin
2 teaspoons cold water

easy lecithin eye cream Melt lanolin in the usual way, add the almond oil, and remove from the heat. Slowly add the powdered lecithin, being careful not to get any lumps, then add the cold water. Mix it all together with either an electric beater or wooden spoon. You have made about 28g (1 oz)of rich, satiny cream, and it takes about five minutes. Although rich it is quite runny so that you do not drag the skin as you might with a thick heavy cream.

This cream is perfect for the delicate eye area as the penetrating almond oil is the finest of oil, the lanolin nourishes and moisturizes, and the lecithin provides protein as well as preventing the cream from going rancid. We don't add any perfume as the eye area is very sensitive and perfume can cause allergies.

The Extra Rich Vitamin Cream on p.49 is also suitable for use as an eye cream.

To relax tension

We use our eyes all day and they get tired and strained from the wind, strong light, reading, watching television and a host of other activities. One way to relax them is by *palming*. Put the base of the palm of your hands over your closed eyes and press gently and firmly. This total blackness is thoroughly relaxing. Another method is to cover your eyes with your cupped hand. Open your eyes and stare into the darkness for a minute. Now relax and do the first palming.

An old-fashioned remedy to cure hysteria was to press under the eyebrow at the bridge of the nose. Use your thumb or little finger and press fairly hard. It hurts, but a tremendous amount of tension does get lodged here and this really does relieve it.

To restore their lustre

eyebright As the name of this herb suggests it is ideal for keeping eyes bright. As Culpeper wrote: 'If this herb was but used as much as it is neglected, it would spoil the spectacle trade of England.'

Use 4 tablespoons of the fresh plant (or 2 tablespoons of the dried herb), and add them to 2 cups of hot water. Let this cool, strain and bottle – and *use*. Bathe your eyes with it often, as it really is a marvellous eye lotion and no house should be without it.

If you cannot get hold of eyebright make an eye lotion from an infusion of rosemary, sage or elderflowers – or even just plain salt and water.

tea It's most likely that our grandmothers used tea as an eye lotion or, by soaking cotton gauze in cold tea, as eye pads. We are much luckier in that all we need to do is soak two tea bags and use them. They fit the eye perfectly and could have been made specifically for this purpose!

cucumber This is also well known as a means of brightening tired eyes. When you next give yourself a mask try using very thin slices on your eyes instead of eyepads. I am always amazed at the way cucumbers are so cold and refreshing, making them ideal for tired, stinging eyes.

mint Culpeper wrote that crushed mint takes away the darkness around the eyes.

potatoes The craziest – and my favourite – eye pads, are made from very thin slices of raw potato. They draw out the puffiness from around the eyes and leave them fresh and clear (to get these paper thin slices I use a potato peeler across the potato).

witch-hazel This can also be used on cotton wool as eye pads, and is very effective for reducing puffiness and redness (but if my eyes are very tired I find it stings slightly).

Eye make-up

Throughout history eye make-up has been of tremendous importance to women everywhere. Ask a woman which make-up she most values and which she would take on a desert island and the answer would be, almost inevitably, her eye make-up.

This was equally true centuries ago. Bilkis, Queen of Saaba, is said to have travelled to the court of King Solomon after she had

heard of his great wisdom. The trip took a long time, but Bilkis was well prepared for the journey – she had one camel-load of eyeshadow. A favourite eye make-up of this beautiful queen was made of powdered pearls and copper sulphate.

kohl This is probably the oldest eye make-up: beautiful kohl containers have been found in the Pyramids. It is still used all over the East and is, I think, one of the best eye cosmetics available. It is used to draw a dark line inside the eye lid, thus giving luminosity to the eyes and outlining them. It is now available in Indian or Oriental shops all over the world and has recently enjoyed great popularity in Europe.

An ancient way of making it was to 'remove the inside of a lemon, fill it up with plumbago and burnt copper, and place it on the fire until it becomes carbonised, then pound it in the mortar with coral, sandalwood, pearls, ambergris, the wing of a bat and part of the body of a burnt chameleon and moistened with rosewater when hot' (Rimmel). Needless to say, I have not made this, and don't worry – the modern version isn't quite as lethal. Some modern kohl is made from antimony which dilates the pupils. Large pupils are supposed to show that you trust someone, so perhaps that was why antimony was first used.

How to make your eyelashes grow

Many women I have met are quite sure that if you apply vaseline to your eyelashes each night it makes them grow. Personally I have not noticed any improvement when I tried, but maybe you will be luckier.

'Those who look into her eyes become enchanted, as wine enchants the reasoning of the drinker.'

Umar Ibn Umar, Qadi of Cordoba and Seville in the time of the Almohades

TEETH

In Sarawak, black teeth were considered beautiful and people rubbed them with burnt coconut shells powdered and mixed with oil. This prevented them, it was said, from looking like dogs! We, however, have not taken 'black is beautiful' that far and still consider that teeth should be gleaming white and pearly.

Teeth,. nails and hair are all formed from the same substance – protein (our teeth are believed to be direct descendents of our scales when we lived in the sea) – and diet plays an essential part in their health. Phosphorous, calcium and vitamins A and D are most important and are contained in butter, milk, cheese, fish, fruit and vegetables; whereas sugar, sweets, soft drinks and snacks are all most undesirable (the sugar sticks to the teeth giving it time to ferment and encourage bacteria). I was told in Morocco that sunflower seeds are very good for your teeth and that they will cure, or prevent, bleeding gums. This is very likely because sunflower seeds are rich in the necessary vitamins and minerals, which just goes to show how much truth there is in so many of these old beliefs.

Apart from diet, how can we look after our teeth? The most important thing is to keep them really clean. Every time you talk, smile, laugh or scream, your teeth are going to be visible, so you would think we would bother to look after them properly. It is surprising, however, how little attention we give to them, apparently thinking that a hasty scrub morning and evening is enough – it isn't.

They should be cleaned at least two or three times a day with a different brush each time to allow the brushes to dry. But do you know how to clean them properly? Most of us use too much toothpaste and tend to think that if our mouth feels fresh from the peppermint or menthol flavouring in the toothpaste, our teeth are clean – the chances are that they are not. We should brush with

an up-and-down movement and clean a couple of teeth at a time starting at the back. Most dentists agree that electric toothbrushes are a good idea – probably because, as they work so quickly, the average two minutes we spend cleaning our teeth will be more effective than two minutes with an ordinary toothbrush.

There are two oral problems, dental decay and gum disease. Both of these are caused basically by 'plaque', the soft white material which builds up on the teeth between cleaning. If not removed in its early stages, by brushing, this plaque hardens to form 'calcus' which has to be removed by the dentist during scaling.

Dental decay develops from the contact of sugar with the teeth and plaque. This sugar is converted by the plaque bacteria into acid thus producing decay. Gum disease is caused by the plaque bacteria penetrating the fine, delicate skin of the gums, causing inflammation. Gum disease varies from, in its mild form, simple gum inflammation, to bleeding or receding gums and, in its extreme form, loss of teeth. These conditions arise from inefficient cleaning of the teeth and can be prevented and cured by regular and effective brushing.

If we can control plaque, we are on our way to keeping our teeth and gums healthy. This regular tooth brushing is essential. Brushing with water alone is quite effective but toothpaste hinders the build-up of stain on the teeth and if it is a fluoride paste, also helps to reduce decay. Toothpicks and dental floss are a great asset and should be used in this fight against plaque. (Roman women used toothpicks of mastic wood to harden their gums and sweeten their breath).

Unfortunately, for years the dentist has had a bad reputation, and some people are still so frightened of the dentist that they would rather wait and risk eventually having to have all their teeth removed than go for regular check-ups. Nowadays there is absolutely no reason to be scared of the dentist as, with anaesthetics and tranquillizers, treatments are absolutely painless. And the most valuable recipe I can give for healthy teeth is to brush them thoroughly after each meal and to go to the dentist for regular check-ups.

'To make the teeth of children grow hastily, seethe hare's brain and annoint therewith the gums . . . and it shall make them grow without any sorrow or disease or aching' (English *Leechbook* of the fifteenth century). Far safer than this recipe, however, would be to take your child to an orthodontist. An orthodontist checks whether the bite is correct, if the teeth are balanced or overcrowded and whether a brace is necessary. It is much easier to correct any faults when you are young: think how unfortunate it would be for a woman to wear a brace when she is trying to look beautiful.

I am constantly amazed to see people who are obviously beauty-conscious and spend money on clothes, and yet have discoloured, misshapen teeth. I would save for years to have my teeth improved, as I think nothing is so obvious or ageing. A well-known film make-up artist told me that if an actor or actress looks too young you simply have to put a brown stain on their teeth and it will age them ten years. What a horrifying thought – and so here are some recipes to whiten your teeth.

Tooth powders
All sorts of odd and peculiar things have been used for cleaning the teeth, but there are some ingredients and recipes that recur and are used in all parts of the world.

This is a combination that I use and can highly recommend:

3 tablespoons bicarbonate of soda
2 tablespoons salt

Keep it in a pot and use it as you would any commercial tooth powder. A friend of mine who smokes a lot swears by this recipe as it has removed all the nicotine stains from her teeth. Plain salt could also be used but this mixture is more effective. You can add pulverized orange and lemon peel to the mixture to whiten the teeth (or use the peels by themselves). I have also found that ashes of burnt bread, charcoal, burnt rosemary and a mixture of honey and salt and rye meal are effective. But these are rather fiddly to make and not as good as our basic bicarbonate and salt.

Strawberries can also be used to clean teeth. Simply rub one over your teeth and this not only polishes them, but tastes delicious.

Many old herbals state that to rub the teeth with a sage leaf makes them white, healthy and pearly. In the same fifteenth-century *Leechbook* as above, I found this recipe for 'yellow teeth, rotten and stinking'. 'Take sage and stamp it in a mortar and put thereto as much salt, make little pastilles and put them into an oven till they be black and burnt. And with that rub well the teeth and it shall do away the corruption and make them fair teeth and good.'

Another effective power is made by burning a couple of slices of bread and pounding them into a fine powder. Flavour this charcoal with a few drops of clove or peppermint oil and use as a tooth powder. If you use this daily you will be amazed at how clean it makes your teeth. I met a gypsy recently who is a regular user of this powder and, in spite of her age, sixty-three, her teeth are amazingly healthy and white.

Toothsticks

In many parts of the world people use sticks to clean their teeth. One end of these toothsticks is peeled and chewed until it becomes soft, just like a toothbrush. In the 'civilised' countries, we tend to use too much toothpaste, and to get the whole cleaning process over in less than a minute – all we have done is given ourselves a nice fresh taste in our mouths. With a stick, however, you spend a long time rubbing up and down, the bristles clear away the plaque, massage the gums and leave the teeth smooth, white and gleaming.

Whenever I go to Kenya I always come back with a large supply of African toothsticks known as 'Mswaki', which the Arabs call 'Maswak'. The Africans at the coast and in the desert use Mswaki and they have marvellously white teeth. My teeth are never as clean as when I have been using sticks – maybe because for once I have to spend some time on them. Just keep the stick with you and use it at odd moments: it is nice to have something to fiddle with, especially if you have just given up smoking. I was most amused, recently, to find a toothpaste allegedly containing the 'bark of African trees' – so there really might be something in the sticks to whiten the teeth.

If African toothsticks are not available try using the (wooden) end of a match, but be gentle and take care not to damage your gums. Or, better still, use medicated tooth picks which are available from the chemist.

Mouth washes

The simplest and best is rosewater. Another very refreshing, easy one, is a strong infusion of mint. Less pleasant tasting, but one which is most effective especially if you suffer from bleeding gums, is a salt and water solution mixed with a few drops of peroxide. This will help to keep the teeth free from infection and whiten them.

Cloves are also used to sweeten the breath, either chewed by themselves or added to this lotion (which is adapted from a recipe 'To keep the teeth both white and sound' in a lovely book called *Delights for Ladies*, 1609).

Boil them all together and 'wash your teeth therewith'. A few drops of myrrh can be added to this last mouth wash, or just added to plain water and used by itself as a mouth wash. Myrrh has disinfectant properties and is reputed to help cure spongy, bleeding gums. It smells exotic too.

1/4 cup vinegar
1/2 cup wine
1/4 cup honey
1 teaspoon powdered cloves

False teeth

Nowadays you could have totally false teeth and no one would know – very different from the last century. Some false wooden teeth, known as Waterloo teeth, were discovered on the battlefields, and it is reported that some actually rooted! Other false teeth were made from very heavy porcelain and even stainless steel – imagine the shock you would get if someone smiled and exposed a mouthful of shiny, stainless steel teeth! Although, I suppose this is no different to my surprise and amusement while in Istanbul recently, where my taxi-driver had a complete set of gold teeth – obviously a lucrative job!

The story goes that a certain Mid-European diplomat had to have all his teeth removed and while waiting for false teeth to be made, he was lent the Ambassador's spare set. The poor diplomat had to wear them – despite the fact they were terribly uncomfortable – as he was expected to consider it a great honour to be lent the Ambassador's teeth.

'To blush and gently smile.'

Herrick

HAIR

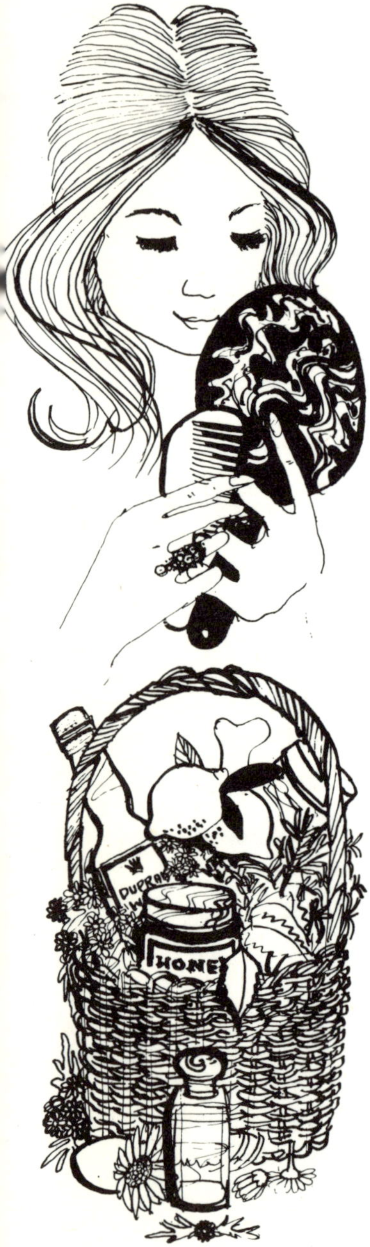

Beautiful, shining hair is, traditionally, a woman's crowning glory, and women everywhere have probably spent more, both in time and money, on their hair than on any other part of their bodies. Such healthy, luxurious hair is not really all that difficult to achieve, but it does take a little time and knowledge.

Although the hair we see is dead (only the root is growing) it still tends to be a barometer of your general state of health. If you are healthy the chances are that your hair will look good; but if you are overworked, tense or ill, your hair will instantly reflect it, tension in the hair follicle muscle being influenced by health. Hair is fed by the blood flowing to the follicle so that is why diet and good circulation are vital to healthy hair. Since hair is formed mostly of protein, known as keratin, a high protein diet is one of the first steps to take. Eat lots of lean meat – especially liver, which is high in iron – seafood, which contains all-important iodine, and lots of fresh vegetables and fruit.

A hair forms, grows, and pushes out of a tiny follicle underneath the scalp, and because your scalp is a continuation of your face it needs the same attention. A healthy scalp produces healthy hair so it must be cleaned, oiled and massaged, in exactly the same way as your face. Hair grows at the rate of half an inch a month, a little faster in warm weather, which is why you may easily have more hair on the side of your head that you sleep on, the heat having stimulated growth.

The life span of each hair can be anything from several years to a few months depending on how it is treated. And don't be alarmed at all those hairs in your hairbrush, as a normal scalp loses about fifty hairs a day, and replaces them. In autumn and spring this turnover increases, because like animals, we moult, so that this is a good time to take a course of yeast tablets (in France Vitamin B tablets are especially sold for this moulting period).

Vets give yeast to show-animals to get their coats to shine; similarly trichologists and hairdressers give it to clients having hair-conditioning treatments. It really does help, so do try it. Brewers' yeast tablets are what you want, the dosage depending on the individual, but anything from two upwards per day (one hairdresser recommends six daily).

Massage

Leading trichologists recommend frequent massage of the scalp – which will help make hair grow faster. Massage certainly loosens the scalp and improves the circulation, hence encouraging growth and giving elasticity to the hair.

Start massaging with the fingers together at the top of your head, using the cushions not the tips, or you might scratch yourself with your nails. Make rotary movements, working over the entire scalp, and *moving the scalp, not the fingers*. Once you have mastered this you will find it so easy and relaxing that you will probably do it at every spare moment – on the bus, watching TV – the more the better.

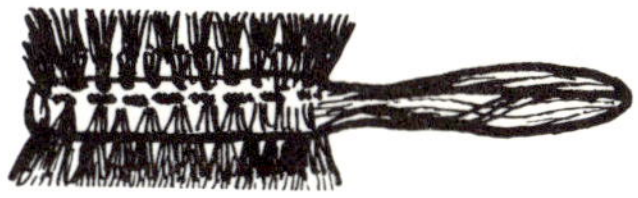

Brushing

The old maxim that the way to healthy hair was to brush it a hundered times a day is now under dispute. Some experts say it makes hair greasier and encourages split ends, while other recommend brushing as often as possible with a soft bristle brush. The truth is that you should try both methods and use the one that suits you best. If you are going to brush, brush with your head hanging down, which gives bounce to the hair and increases circulation – and also, incidentally, exercises the bosom, thus killing three birds with one stone!

The circulation can also be increased by standing on your head. By now you must be rather bored of me telling you to do headstands, but all that blood rushing to your face and scalp will do wonders for your skin and hair.

Shampoos

The thing to remember when shampooing your hair is to take care. During the washing process, you loosen the old hairs which are ready to fall out (so don't worry about all those hairs in the basin), but wet hair is extremely vulnerable, becoming very stretchy and easily broken, so treat it with respect.

All shampoos are basically detergents which, if used over-lavishly, can strip the hair of its natural oils, drying the scalp and causing it to flake. A famous New York hairdresser recommends always diluting half the amount of shampoo you would normally use with water and beating it up with an egg beater before using it. She suggests rinsing your hair through first and only giving it one really thorough shampoo (this depends, however, on the greasiness of the hair). It is much better to wash your hair slightly more often following this method, or simply to use a mild shampoo as this will allow the hair to retain some of its natural protective oils.

After washing your hair don't instantly start to brush it. Wrap it in a towel and blot out some of the moisture; rubbing splits the ends, and immediately tugging at very wet hair, in its weakened state, pulls out the hair. When a hair is yanked out, as opposed to falling out naturally, it could take as long as 3 months before the hair follicle starts to grow a replacement (a good reason to treat your hair with respect). When your hair is slightly dry comb it with a wide-toothed comb, starting from the ends, slowly working up to the crown. In this way you avoid tangles and excess pulling.

egg shampoo This must be one of the oldest beauty recipes, as references can be found in every beauty book I have ever read. Eggs are full of protein, and they are still as effective a treatment today as they have obviously been throughout history.

In its most basic form you simply wash your hair with the egg alone. Beat up one or two eggs with a cup of water and thoroughly massage this into your wet hair, for about five to ten minutes. This will take a little longer than an ordinary shampoo, but it is important that you allow time for the egg to clean the hair, and for the protein contained in the egg to condition the hair. Rinsing it out thoroughly is terribly important, otherwise your hair will feel dank, rather than thick, and not clean and bouncy as it should. And remember not to use hot water, or you will end up with scrambled egg on your head!

1-2 tablespoons clear, cheap shampoo
1 egg

variations on the egg theme Simply beat these together and use. Don't worry about which shampoo to use, anything will do. This version is quicker to use than the last and I consequently much prefer it.

conditioning shampoo Mix all together, beating the gelatine in slowly in order to avoid lumps. The egg and gelatine are both protein so the conditioning effect of this shampoo is fantastic, and it will be most beneficial to damaged or dry hair.

With the egg added the shampoo will go off, which is why I suggest you make just enough to use straight away. But you can make a large batch of the shampoo and gelatine mixture which, when heated slowly over a double boiler or in a water bath, then cooled, will set into a gel making it ideal for travelling and an effective conditioning shampoo (you can always add the egg separately).

Gelatine gives the hair body, making it lovely and thick, and can also be used as a setting lotion (see p.91).

1-2 tablespoons cheap shampoo
1 egg
1 tablespoon unflavoured powder gelatine

herb shampoos These are easy to prepare. Simply make a strong infusion of your favourite herb and add a cupful to your shampoo. Rosemary is the herb most commonly used as it brightens the hair and helps prevent dandruff and hair loss. Other herbs that can be added are thyme, sage, camomile, and yarrow for greasy hair.

Kashmiri protein shampoo Soak a cup of lentils overnight, or for a couple of hours, then liquidize them with enough water to make a paste. Use this paste in the same way you would any ordinary shampoo. I was given this recipe by a Kashmiri girl who always uses it and has the most beautiful and healthy hair. I'm always scared that these old treatments will take all day but I used it a few times and found it every bit as quick and good as a normal shampoo.

When I first heard this recipe I got very enthusiastic and persuaded lots of people to use it. We all found it most effective, and discovered it was especially suitable for fine, fly-away hair as it gives it body.

Pakistani shampoo A Pakistani friend of mine always uses this traditional recipe, and her hair is long, thick and luscious. Her younger sisters laugh at her for using such an old-fashioned recipe, but they have lots of white hairs and she has none!

225g (8 oz) dried olives
225g (8 oz) Sirakai beans

The beans are difficult to obtain, but occasionally I have found them in Indian food shops. Wash the olives and beans in cold water and then soak overnight in an iron pot. The next day boil them for ten to fifteen minutes and strain. Now comes the work of de-seeding them, which is a long job (do it watching television or talking to someone). Liquidize the flesh that remains and use the paste to wash your hair with. This shampoo darkens the hair, especially with repeated use, and leaves it feeling really soft and amazing shiny, so the results make the lengthy preparation worthwhile.

Dry shampoos

powder In many parts of the world the women never, or very rarely, wash their hair. A Chinese friend of mine, for instance, remembers both her grandmother and mother using a very, very fine-toothed comb and combing out the dirt for hours both in the morning and at night (*literally* hours she says). The special lacquer they used on their hair would absorb the grease, so they would only have to comb out the dirt and old lacquer.

In India and other parts of the East it is very common to use an absorbent meal – corn meal or rye meal – to remove all the stale grease and dirt. To clean your hair in this way, simply sprinkle cornflour meal all over the scalp, making partings to get it really everywhere. Leave it on for anything from a few minutes to overnight, then brush it out. Use a soft bristle brush – nylon brushes break the hair – and brush all the meal out *thoroughly* (if you don't your hair will feel heavy and look worse than before). This method of 'shampooing' is very good for your hair as you are not constantly using harsh detergents, and leaves the hair looking really shiny.

If cornmeal is not available use any absorbent powder. Try using the kaolin or Fuller's Earth that I hope you have bought, and are already using in your face masks.

cologne This is marvellous if you are going out unexpectedly, and your hair, especially the front section, looks a bit lank or dirty. Dab some eau de cologne or lavender water on a bristle brush and brush it through your hair. This removes any excess grease and dirt and leaves your hair smelling so good. I find I often resort to this, and sometimes, if my hair is really dirty, I cover the brush with a stocking or a piece of cloth, put the cologne on that and then brush, which is even more effective.

I love the fact that even if your hair wasn't looking very good, you can restore it and smell good with just a few minutes' brushing.

Incense cones

My Pakistani friend also perfumes her hair after washing it; when it is half dry, she burns some incense and lets the smoke go into her damp hair, thus making it smell quite beautiful. She makes her own incense by burning sandalwood and myrrh or by making up this recipe.

6 tablespoons powdered charcoal
5 tablespoons powdered myrrh
1 tablespoon powdered benzoin

2-3 drops oil of bergamot
2-3 drops oil of sandalwood

1 tablespoon potassium nitrate
Mucilage of tragacanth

Mix the powders together and sieve, and then add the oils. Add the potassium nitrate, and then sufficient mucilage of tragacanth to make a stiff paste. Heat the mixture over a water bath and then make into little cones and dry. When you want some incense just light one of the cones; the smell is highly aromatic and exotic.

You could also use incense sticks and cones available from Indian and Oriental shops everywhere.

Rinses

We have already established that rinsing your hair thoroughly after washing is absolutely essential. Rinse with plain water until your hair squeaks. Then by using a final rinse of some other liquid, you help to remove the last traces of soap scum and make the hair infinitely more bouncy and shiny.

For dark hair

The most common rinse is vinegar. Dilute a tablespoon of vinegar, it doesn't matter what sort, and use it in the final rinse. I am often in such a hurry that I used to just pour it on straight from the bottle – but now I keep diluted vinegar in the bathroom all ready. Eight parts water to one part vinegar, and you can use it on your face, your hair, and in your bath. Vinegar is a most valuable beauty aid as it restores the acid mantle, and the smell quickly evaporates leaving your hair soft and full of lights and really shiny. This is particularly useful if soap has been used to wash the hair.

For fair hair

Use diluted lemon juice in your final rinse, about eight parts water to one part lemon juice. It works in the same way as the vinegar, and leaves the hair marvellously shiny.

Herbal rinses

There are hundreds of herbs to choose from, depending on your hair type, which will be extremely effective used in rinses for your hair. Try infusions of sage on dark hair, yarrow on greasy hair, verbena and lavender to make it smell delicious. And, most important, remember when using one of these special rinses, to put a bowl underneath your hair so that you can re-use the water several times.

rosemary According to herbal books rosemary is a cure-all, conditioning, adding lustre, preventing dandruff and falling hair. Make a strong infusion of rosemary, two tablespoons to 2 cups boiling water, strain and use it as a final rinse. This is especially good for dark hair as it brings out the highlights. If you have rosemary oil you can use this instead of the herbal infusion.

camomile This has always been widely used throughout Europe to keep fair hair blonde. I remember my grandmother using it on my sister to try and keep her ever-darkening hair golden. Again make a strong infusion of the dried flowers, about 1-2 tablespoons to 2 cups boiling water, and use it as a final rinse.

catmint This is widely used by the Romany gypsies as a final rinse, and is said to ease irritations of the scalp and stimulate growth.

marigold Use either fresh or dried flower heads. Make a strong infusion using four tablespoons of marigolds to two cups of boiling water or vinegar. Allow the infusion to steep for ten to twenty minutes, strain and use in the final rinse. Poured over the hair several times, it leaves the hair soft, shiny and full of highlights.

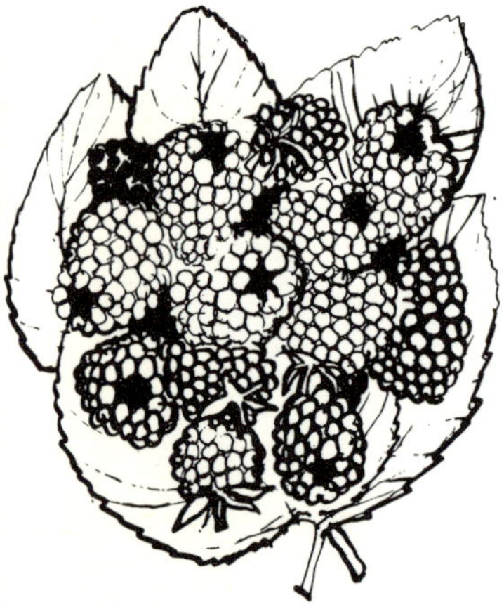

raspberry leaves These are widely used by country women as they act as a disinfectant and normalizer (the leaves, being slightly acid, help restore the acid mantle to the hair).

Dyes

> 'Did I tell you to leave off dyeing your hair?
> Now you have none to dye'.
>
> *Ovid*

Throughout history women have wanted to change the way they look and hair colouring is one way of achieving this. All sorts of peculiar concoctions have been used: walnut shells, acorns and bear's grease, roots, oil of tartar and even the blood of a black bull! In Ancient Rome many of the slave girls had blonde hair which was greatly envied by the fashionable Roman women. They started to try and bleach their own hair the same golden blonde. An Italian monk wrote that 'ladies of Italy are immodest and dishonest for they try to cheat nature herself, spending hours in the sunshine anointing their hair with some secret ointments'. These 'secret ointments' often consisted of sodium carbonate and unslated lime which badly damaged the hair causing it to fall out (thus that poem by Ovid!).

A Turkish women I know once bought some Oil of Bay from a chemist in Kyrenia, Cyprus, who knew she was interested in herbs. 'The villagers use this to keep the colour of their hair,' he said. 'If it is dark, it gets darker, if blonde, blonder!' It did her hair a world of good. Here are some recipes for fair and dark hair whose results I can predict more accurately, and which are less dramatic than the examples quoted above.

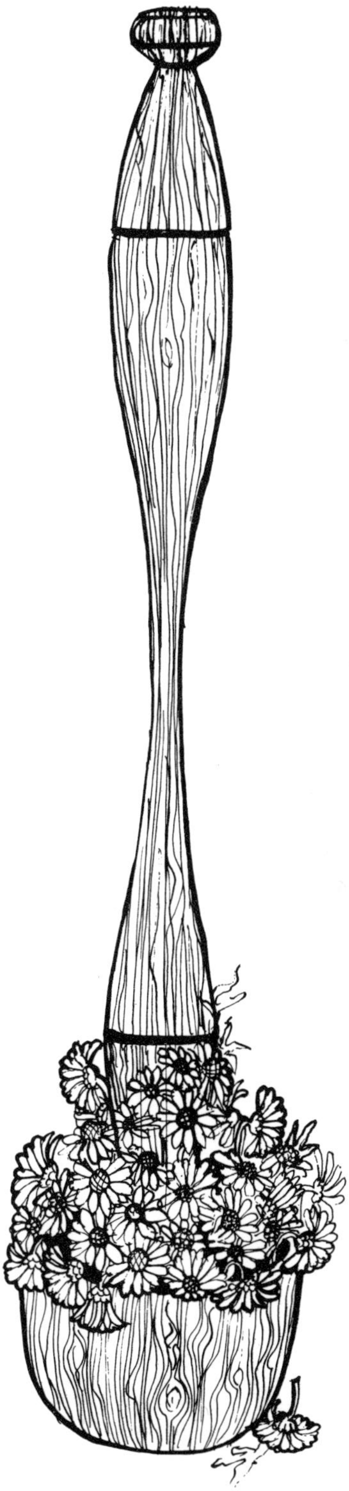

For fair hair
camomile These flowers are world renowned for their bleaching effect. They can be used either as a rinse (just add 2 tablespoons to a pint of water, infuse, and use as your final rinse) or as a dye. For the dye, make a very strong infusion – 4 tablespoons to 1 cup water – and let this stand for at least twenty minutes. Strain, and then mix into a paste with kaolin. Apply this paste to the roots of your hair first, then comb it through. Leave it on for anything from twenty minutes to an hour, depending on the porosity of your hair and the colour you wish it to turn out. The longer you leave it on, obviously, the more it will bleach your hair.

saffron Alexander the Great went to Bactriana during his Afghan campaign and fell in love with a beautiful golden-haired girl, Princess Rusnak, whom he married in great splendour. Her hair was so exquisite that she became known as 'Rusnak of the Shining Plaits'. It is said that she always used saffron to keep its lustre, and also keep the love of the conqueror of the world!

rhubarb 'Besides that it comforteth the brain and memory it maketh the hair long, fair and yellow like gold. Take the rind or scrapings of rhubarb and seepe it in white wine and after you have washed your hair with it, you shall wet your hair with a sponge and let them dry in the sun' (*The Secrets of Master Alexis Piedmontese*, 1555). This rhubarb dye is most effective. Simmer the rhubarb root and stem – about three sticks – in 2 cups either white wine or water, for about half an hour. Remove from the heat, and let it steep for another half an hour, then strain. This liquid can be used as a rinse or mixed with kaolin to form a paste and used as a dye. Leave it on the hair for anything from twenty minutes to an hour, depending on the colour you want. It lightens the hair considerably, and with continued use can make mousey hair a lovely golden shade.

For dark hair

henna The use of henna as a hair dye can be traced back to the Egyptians, and it has been used ever since all over the Middle and Near East. It can either give the hair lovely highlights or turn it bright flaming red. It doesn't change the chemical structure of the hair as chemical dyes do, but simply coats the hair, thus giving it body. With henna it is impossible to predict exactly what colour your hair will turn out – it depends on the texture and colour of your hair – and so I would advise you to dye a cutting of your hair the first time.

There are all sorts of ways of using henna:

1. 1 cup of henna mixed to a paste with 1 cup boiling water.

2. 1 cup of henna mixed to a paste with a cup of strong hot tea (this bring out the red more).

3. 1 cup of henna mixed to a paste with 1 cup of coffee (this dulls down the red slightly).

To any of these henna pastes you can add an egg and a tablespoon of castor oil – as I do – because this counteracts any drying effect the herb might have and also helps the paste stick to the hair better.

Heat the henna paste over a double boiler, let it steep there for anything from ten minutes to half an hour. Cool, then re-heat to boiling point. Remove from the heat (now add the egg and castor oil), and apply as hot as possible. Massage into the scalp, remembering to wear rubber gloves – otherwise you will have bright red hands for the next few days. If the ends of your hair are dry, they will be more porous and turn brighter faster, so don't comb the henna through until towards the end of the dyeing time. Wrap in a large scarf, towel, or plastic bag and let the henna do its work. (You can also wrap your hair in tinfoil which keeps the heat in and makes the dye work quicker.) Leave it on for anything from fifteen minutes to three hours. Then wash it off.

In the Middle East and Morocco I have seen children with henna packs left on their heads all day, but I usually leave it on for about three quarters of an hour to get a really rich colour.

Henna not only colours the hair but also conditions and thickens it. It can also be used as a rinse: make an infusion of the powder (one tablespoon to half a pint of water) and rinse your hair with it. In the East it is also used to calm down fevers, when a paste is placed on the palms and feet to cool them. Many woman henna their hands and feet with intricate designs: this could have originated as a cooling device, and has now become a recipe for beauty.

But *never* use henna on top of chemical dyes as it can cause a reaction. If in doubt go to your hairdresser.

sage If your hair is going grey try darkening it with sage leaves. Make a strong infusion with the leaves, about 4 tablespoons to 1 cup water. Apply this water to the roots each day and you will soon see a result. When the desired colour is obtained use it only once a week.

The other way to use sage is to mix this infusion with kaolin to make a paste. Apply this to the hair and leave it on about half an hour then wash it off. To increase the darkening effect of sage mix it with tea instead of water.

hibiscus flowers In Kashmir they rinse their hair with a strong infusion of hibiscus flowers to bring out the red highlights (a handful of hibiscus flowers to a pint of boiling water). This sounds lovely and exotic but unfortunately is one of the few things I have been unable to try due to the lack of hibiscus flowers in this country.

red oak bark Once when I could not buy henna a Frenchwoman suggested I try red oak bark. Her mother always used it and at the age of seventy had no white hairs. Make an infusion in the usual way and rinse your hair in it. It gives a lovely dark sheen.

indigo leaves In the Middle East indigo leaves were used to give the hair a blue-black lustre, but as Saadi said, 'It is useless to use indigo leaves on a bald man's brow'.

Hair problems

Dandruff

Most people suffer from this at some time in their lives. It is usually a reflection of health, over-tiredness, tension, bad diet or even excessive use of harsh shampoos which dry out the scalp. It is best controlled by diet: eat masses of lean meat, fresh fruit and vegetables and avoid all those chocolates, cakes and fat which make the circulation sluggish. Keep your hair clean and with a good healthy diet, lots of brushing, massage, herbal tonics and rinses, you should be able to cure your dandruff quickly. If it persists go to a trichologist.

nettle tonic Nettles are renowned for their properties as a hair tonic, and for preventing dandruff. Infuse a handful of nettle leaves in one pint of boiling water and use this infusion as the final rinse. If you already have dandruff, however, make a strong infusion of nettles to which add half a cup of vinegar. Massage this mixture into your scalp night and morning and you will find your dandruff will soon disappear. Do remember to massage it in well, as this is an important part of the treatment.

Conditioners

As I've said, hair reflects one's general health; tension, overwork and illness all can affect your hair, so if your complaint is really bad and persists, go to the doctor or a trichologist. Short hair is normally healthier than long hair, for the simple reason that it is younger. Long hair may have been in the scalp for as long as six to eight years; being so far from the hair follicle, which lubricates the hair, the ends tend to get dry and split. And this is why we need conditioners.

The best conditioners I know are massage and (yet again!) headstands. All the recipes I give here will work best if *well* massaged into the scalp.

for dry damaged hair Heat some oil and massage it into the scalp. Wrap your head in a warm towel and leave it on for half an hour. An ideal time to do this treatment is if you ever go and have a sauna, or steam bath. I sometimes put a plastic bag over my head and then a scarf as this retains the heat and aids absorption of the oil. Wash it off with a mild shampoo. Follow this process with any of the following oil suggestions or recipes and you will soon notice an improvement.

Coconut oil is used by Indian and Mexican women who all have tremendously long, beautiful hair. Olive and castor oils are also widely used. A few years ago in America there was a tremendous craze for using mayonnaise – it contains all these required nutritious ingredients and is marvellous.

a conditioner to keep Melt the oils in one pan and mix the waters together in another pan, and heat both over a water bath. Hold on the heat for a minute to ensure they are both hot, then remove. Quickly add the water to the oils, continously beating with your beater on low until they are thoroughly mixed. When it cools, you may find that the cream has separated, but don't worry as you can just beat it up again with your beater on high. These ingredients give you a large pot of very nutritious conditioning cream.

2 tablespoons lanolin
3 tablespoons castor oil
½ tablespoon coconut oil
1 tablespoon vegetable lard

½ cup water
1 teaspoon vinegar
1 teaspoon glycerine
1 teaspoon liquid soap (or clear shampoo)

To use this cream, apply 2 tablespoons to your dry hair and steam it in. You can make it even more nutritious by adding an egg – which makes a really fresh, conditioning hair cream. And the cream is amazing, for within a couple of applications it will restore lustre even to the worst, dry, sun-bleached hair.

quick hair conditioner Hair conditioners are just as important for men, especially now that men have longer hair. Recently I had a telephone call in the middle of the night from a frantic actor who was doing a modelling job the next day and wanted to know how to make his hair really shiny. This was the recipe I gave him.

1 egg
2 tablespoons castor oil
1 teaspoon vinegar
1 teaspoon glycerine

Mix these together with an electric or hand beater. Massage into the scalp, steam or wrap your head in a scarf and hot towel, then wash off. I use castor oil in these recipes as it hardens slightly when exposed to the air, thus adding body. You will find that after using either of these last two conditioners your hair will be left looking thicker, more shiny, soft and manageable.

honey conditioner Mix these ingredients together and massage them well into the scalp. Steam the hair, then shampoo. This leaves the hair very easy to manage and it stays looking lovely for days instead of becoming limp once the set has gone. Especially good for fine hair with a tendency to dryness.

1 egg
1 teaspoon honey
2 teaspoons oil (coconut or olive)

for thinning or listless hair If your hair is in really bad condition and you seem to be losing more than usual, try this ancient Persian treatment. Scoop out the marrow from a large bone, melt it and massage the resulting oily fat into the scalp each night for a week or two. Wrap your head in a scarf to protect the pillow and wash off in the morning. This is a very messy and somewhat smelly treatment but the ensuing results make it worthwhile. The woman who told me of it had used it with great success when living in Persia; her hair was thinning and falling out at an alarming rate, and she said that after only a few days she could see the improvement. There are also many references to it in

English and French books of the seventeenth century (although they were more refined, and strained the bone-marrow through a muslin bag and scented it before use!).

Bone-marrow is a highly nutritious, extremely rich protein, which is why it is so good for hair. I have often used this treatment, especially when by the sea. It counteracts the drying elements of sun and salt, and as I was always washing my hair to get the salt out, it seemed a perfect time to try it. The results were terrific, and well worth any rude comments friends made about a continually turbaned head of hair.

a gypsy hair tonic This is most effective for those losing their hair. Steep a medium sized onion, cut into slices, in half a cup of rum. Leave them for twenty-four hours. Then remove the onions and use the remaining liquid. Massage a little of this into the scalp. Use it each night at first, and then once a week until your condition is remedied.

1 egg
2 tablespoons brandy

another alcoholic conditioner Beat up the egg and brandy, massage into the scalp, leave for 10 minutes and rinse off. This is simple and most effective, the egg nourishing and the brandy stimulating. If, by some lucky chance, you've made too much, drink it – it's just like an egg-nog!

Setting lotions and lacquers

All sort of odd and peculiar things are used as setting lotions: beer, milk, gelatine, lemons.

beer This is probably the most effective and popular. Simply wet the hair with beer (fresh or flat), and set the hair. It gives added body and helps the set stay in. Milk can be used in the same way.

lemon juice This makes a good setting lotion, too, especially for fair or greasy hair. Squeeze a lemon and use the strained juice to obtain a very firm set. When you take out the curlers the hair feels quite hard but when brushed it feels soft and looks very shiny. Lemon juice dries fairly fast and if you put it in a spray bottle it can also be used as an effective hair lacquer. You can make another lemon hair lacquer by cutting up a lemon and boiling it with 1 cup hot water until you have only half a cup left. Strain and use. This lacquer is faster drying and slightly thicker than plain lemon juice. A few drops of alcohol (vodka) should be added to preserve it.

gelatine As it is a protein gelling agent, gelatine is excellent for a setting lotion, giving body to limp hair. Dissolve about 2 tablespoons gelatine in 2 cups boiling water, and use it as the final rinse.

sugar Simply add 1 tablespoon sugar to a glass of boiling water and when it has dissolved use it as a setting lotion. To use it as a lacquer put it into a spray bottle and spray!

'chinese lacquer' In China hair lacquer was a necessity, as it took hours to arrange the elaborate hair styles which would sometimes be kept in for two or three days. Until quite recently some women used lacquer made from wood shavings; these were soaked in water overnight, and the translucent sticky fluid that rose to the surface would be used as lacquer. It was applied with a brush that looked just like a denture brush. A Chinese friend of mine remembers her mother having to get up at four o'clock in the morning to do her hair for a special occasion and apply this lacquer to keep it in place.

hair setting lotion Crush the gum tragacanth with a pestle and mortar, add the water, and stir until the gum dissolves and you have a smooth solution. Now add the alcohol and glycerine. After a couple of hours the lotion will thicken, and you will have a setting lotion every bit as good as any you could buy.

1 teaspoon gum tragacanth
8 tablespoons water

1 tablespoon alcohol
½ teaspoon glycerine

brilliantine Many men use brilliantine and it is very easy to make. Why not pamper the man in your life and make him some.

1 tablespoon castor oil
1 tablespoon coconut oil
1 tablespoon petroleum jelly (vaseline)
1 teaspoon emulsifying wax

Perfume

Melt the ingredients together over a water bath. Remove from the heat, add perfume if desired, beat together with your beater on low speed, and you have made brilliantine. You can change this recipe by simply adding 2 teaspoons of lanolin to the above when melting, and when removed from the heat just mix in 1 teaspoon of water. Then stir intermittently with a wooden spoon while the mixture is cooling.

This brilliantine holds even the most unruly hair in place making it extremely manageable.

'The golden hair that Salle wears
Is hers, who would have thought it!
She swears 'tis hers, and true she swears
For I know where she bought it.'

Mastiel

'Whoever is endowed with beauty,
Wherever he places his foot hands are held out to receive it.'

Saadi

The Body

THE FIGURE AND ITS CARE

Exercise

No matter what shape or size your figure is, it can always benefit by some form of exercise. Exercise makes us agile, tones up the body, improves the circulation, generally wakes up the whole system and makes us feel more alive and much healthier.

Both men and women of all ages look infinitely better with firm bodies, and it is really only exercise which provides just that. Somehow we must try to fit exercise of some sort or other into our daily routine. We could walk instead of taking the car or bus, at least half the way to work, go swimming, or just do the simple limbering-up exercises I describe below. In Brazil, for instance, everyone exercizes madly on the beaches (none of this lazy lying around sunbathing), and if you go to the beach at 6.30 in the morning, it will be full of men doing their daily exercises before going to work.

Stretching

This keeps your body firm and graceful. Imagine that you are an elastic band being stretched to the limit. Watch a cat and see how she stretches every muscle of her body.

Before you get up in the morning lie on top of the bed and gently stretch, first one side then the other. Pull up with the right side, pull down with the left. Now with the other side. Then, out of bed, stand with your feet flat on the ground and reach for the ceiling. Try and touch it. Stretch one side, feel the pull from your fingertips to your feet, now stretch the other side. Do this twelve times, and then do the same stretch standing on your toes – stretch, stretch, stretch. After at least ten times, let your whole body flop, your fingers hanging down to your ankles. Swing gently from side to side, and be floppy just like a rag doll.

Breathing

Every tissue in our body needs oxygen, so be sure to get plenty of fresh air. Start the day by doing some deep breathing in front of an open window. Fill your lungs and slowly exhale, pushing out the last breath. In, out, in, out, slowly and deeply. Repeat about ten times. Now you are ready to face the world.

Deportment

What an old-fashioned word that is, but how vitally important. One of the first things you notice about anyone is the way they carry themselves. So many people stand and walk badly, which not only looks terrible, but can also lead to back problems.

Stand and walk regally. Imagine that a string is coming out of the top of your head and pulling you up, and then the whole body naturally falls into place. In the last century girls used to be made to walk around with books on their heads and not so long ago I remember my grandmother marching us around the room like that. I even remember trying to have tea with those books still precariously balanced there!

To stand properly you need a strong, flexible spine and here is a marvellous exercise. Lie on the floor with your knees bent and feet on the floor and arms by your side. Contract your stomach and you will find your pelvis moves up. Tip your pelvis up and down. Now do the same with the small of your back. Push the small of your back down into the floor, relax and push up and down. This improves the flexibility of the back, strengthens it, and what could be easier? You can also do this exercise sitting up against the wall, or against the back of your chair in the office (even sitting in the underground if you can take the funny looks you might get!).

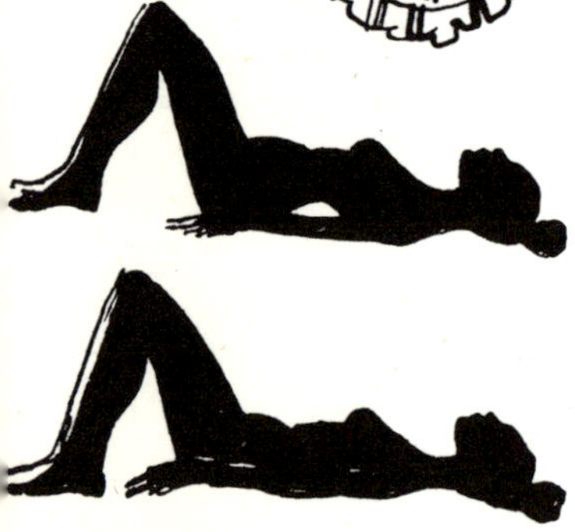

The headstand

The headstand, as you may have gathered by now, should be included in your daily exercise routine. It is one of the most perfect beauty treatments, and well-known in yoga for toning the mind and body. All that blood rushing to your head clears the brain, increases the circulation and is the best tonic your facial muscles, skin and hair can have. It is an instant rejuvenator and reviver from fatigue after a tiring day.

One nonagenarian Hollywood film star was asked how she stayed looking so young with her bright, shiny skin. Her reply was simple: 'I stand on my head for a few minutes each day and have been doing so for the last fifty years.'

The shoulder-stand

If you cannot manage a headstand try doing another yoga exercise – the shoulder-stand or 'plough', which is amazingly relaxing, reviving, stretching, and even, if done often, slims down the hips and abdomen (as well as ankles and calves).

Lie on your back, lift up your legs and body so that you are resting on your shoulders. Now try to lower your legs backwards until your feet are resting behind your head so that you look like a triangle. This might make your shoulders slightly stiff at first, but will soon wear off if you do it regularly.

So next time you are exhausted don't lie down and go to sleep: revitalize yourself with a head- or shoulder-stand. In fact as I write I am vowing to have a campaign and do them each morning.

The slant-board

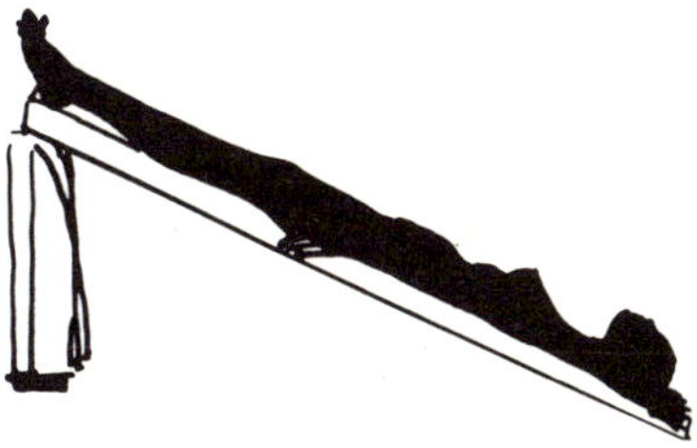

In India there is now a craze of using anti-gravity slant boards, which work on the same principle as our head- or shoulder-stand – but you just lie on a board so it is easier. To make your own slant board, lean an ironing board against a low bed or chair, making sure to wedge it in well and safely, and lie on it with your feet higher than your head and your body at an angle. All the blood that has settled in your legs will rush to your head, thus improving your circulation, resting your muscles and nerves, and after about ten minutes you will feel completely rejuvenated.

Bicycling

Recent research on coronary heart attacks has found that cycling is one of the best forms of exercise. It can minimize the likelihood of having a heart attack by increasing the blood circulation, and exercizing all the muscles, but isn't too strenuous. I am a great believer in the bicycle as it is so exhilarating: and an easy, painless, and useful way of exercizing. To be honest, I often find it much *quicker* and *easier* to use my bicycle than my car!

Skipping

Skipping is a marvellous form of exercise, and unlike so many others, is great fun. It exercises the whole body, especially the upper arms, improves the posture and breathing, and relieves tension. The advantage of skipping is that you can do it almost anywhere, fast or slow, to music or singing those rhymes which everybody knows. And it's fun, and as it's invigorating, gives you energy.

Exercises

Apart from the general limbering-up exercises, I am also including some more specific ones for each part of the body. Although it is theoretically possible to lose weight by exercizing, you have to do so much just to lose a single pound that it is impractical. What it does do is to firm and tone the muscles, giving your figure the illusion of slimness and perfect proportions. As you can concentrate on your problem areas it is the best way to get rid of those bulges.

I am always badgering my clients to do ten minutes' exercise each day. This regularity undeniably pays off and with those who manage it the results make the effort really worthwhile. But for some of us this routine is never achieved. We start off madly keen, then something upsets our routine; oh well, we think, I'll do extra tomorrow. Tomorrow comes and somehow again there is no time and, alas, our resolutions and our exercises are put aside. This happened to me so often that I realized I could never manage it; now I do a really hard, fast work-out for about half an hour to pop music once or twice a week. I find this great fun and probably because I do enjoy it so, somehow manage to keep to it quite faithfully.

Fortunately for us, fashions and figures are nowadays comparatively natural. We want to be slim but we do not have the rigid fashions of the Victorians. Then the hourglass figure was so fashionable that women even used to have their floating ribs removed to achieve it – a highly expensive and dangerous operation. But then, one had to suffer to be beautiful, as this story, reported by Le Follet in 1859, shows: Madame Virginie de C., at twenty-three years old, a young and elegant society woman of the Second Empire in France, had an excessively small waist which gave a striking effect to her crinoline. At a ball one night other women were scarcely able to conceal their jealousy and she looked at her rivals with a disdainful smile. A day or two later she was dead. An autopsy showed that she had been so tightly corseted that three of her ribs had pierced her liver!

Luckily we don't have to go to these tragic extremes, so here are some exercises which I find particularly easy and effective. And whenever you can squeeze them in – do try them, or at least some of them. You can do them when you get up in the morning, after work or before you go to bed: they cannot completely re-shape you, nothing can do that, but if you do them regularly a slimmer, sleeker, super-fit body will emerge.

Arms

The top of the arm is an area which tends to get flabby, so keep an eye on it.

1. An easy exercise to correct this is to stand with your feet apart in a doorway. Clench your fists and raise your arms high overhead against the door-frame. Inhale deeply and press as hard as possible against the frame.

2. Swinging your arms requires no energy and is effective. Rotate them, first forward and then backwards as high as possible.

3. Sit on an ordinary kitchen chair with your feet on the ground and your arms straight down behind you; have your hands flat on the seat with your fingers facing the front. Press on your hands, so that they lift you out of the seat and your feet off the ground. Hold this position for a count of four and lower yourself as slowly as possible – a count of six if you can. Repeat.

Bust

Whether it is fashionable to have a bosom or not does not alter the fact that what one has should be high and firm.

The bosom itself has no muscle, but is supported by the surrounding muscles of the shoulder, back and chest, and it is these muscles which should be exercized.

1. These two exercises are easy, well-known and efficient. With elbows out, press hands together at waist level for count of ten and then at bust level. Relax and repeat. And, press your hands against a wall. Hold the pressure to a count of ten, relax and repeat.

2. Lie on the floor with your arms up straight in the air. Cross them in a scissor movement. You can feel it pulling. Remember to keep your arms straight.

3. The easiest and most relaxing of all is to roll your shoulders slowly, making a large circle; first forwards, then backwards. This is also very good for relieving fibrositis and easing stiff shoulders.

Stomach

The stomach is one of the most obvious problem areas, and unless you want to be corseted, you need to get your own muscles to do the work for you. The only way to achieve this is by exercise.

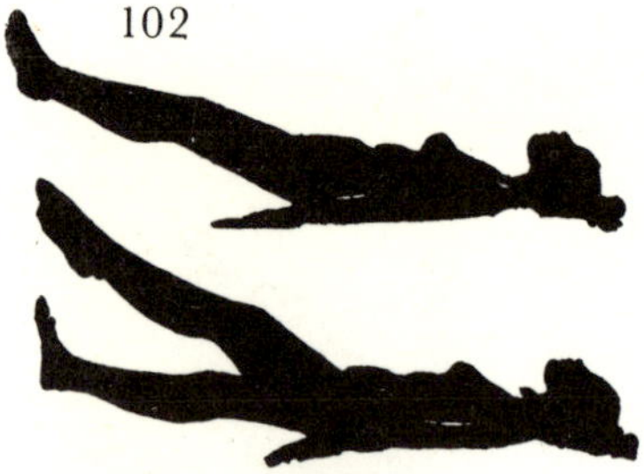

1. Lie on your back, feet together and arms by your sides and the small of your back pressed down. Slowly lift your legs to a height of six inches above the ground. Hold this position, then lower slowly to the count of six, increasing it as your muscles get stronger. Repeat often.

2. Again lying in the same position, this time lift one leg at a time in a scissor movement, not letting your feet touch the ground. If you are doing this correctly you can feel the muscles really working.

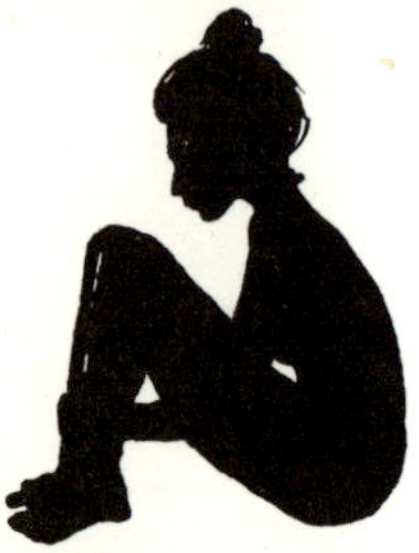

3. Again lying on the floor but this time with your knees bent and your feet on the floor. Slowly raise your head and shoulders to try to reach your knees. Hold and lower your body slowly – the slower the exercise is done the better.

4. Kneel with your hands in front of you on the floor. Lift and extend one leg and then draw it in, trying to touch your forehead with your knee. Do this four times, then repeat with the other leg. In the same position work your tummy muscles, suck them in, blow them out; in, out, in, out. This is one of the best exercises to regain the use of your muscles after pregnancy.

5. A simple exercise to get all your muscles working is to stand with your legs apart and hands above your head. Keeping your knees straight, circle to the right, then left. Try to touch the ground each time and change direction there. This is a very rhythmic exercise and one of my favourites as it's such fun to do.

6. Another rhythmic exercise for the whole torso. Lie flat on the floor, arms out above your head, lift up your torso bringing your arms out to touch your toes, your head as close to your knees as possible. Now roll back gently and lift your legs up to go behind your head into a shoulder stand. Relax down to the starting position. When you master this exercise, it is easy and gets its own rhythm so that it requires very little effort, although you might be going quite fast.

Waistline

These are designed to make your waist supple and flexible.

1. Stand with your legs apart and with the right arm relaxed by your side, and the left arm resting on your head. Bend to the right as far as you can. Repeat this six times to the right and then six times to the left.

2. Stand with your legs apart, point your left foot, and push your right hip and diaphragm out to the right; lift the right arm and incline it to the left leg. Repeat this four times on each side.

3. Lie on your back with your arms outstretched. Lift your right leg and draw a half-circle to the left arm, without moving your body. Repeat this with your right leg. This exercise is also good for the leg muscles.

4. Sit on the floor with legs outstretched to the sides. Lift your arms above your head, bend your body so that your hands reach to your feet and your forehead touches your knee, bounce there four times, lift and repeat on the other side. Now bend over with your hands still reaching for your toes but now attempting to touch your knees with your ear.

Hips

Princess Zuleika was to marry a man she could not bear to come near her, so she invented a story that she had glass hips and would crumble into pieces if she were touched. Today in Afghanistan, if they want to suggest a girl is unapproachable, they say she has glass hips! Our hips, sadly, tend far more towards rotundity and solidity than her fragility; here are some exercises that will fine your hips down.

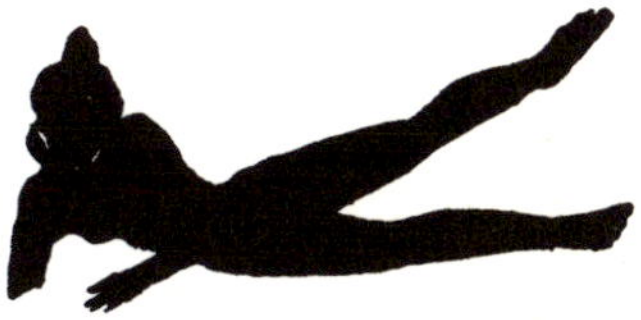

1. Lie on your right side with your head supported by your upstretched right arm, the left hand resting on the ground with your hips well forward and your body in a straight line. Lift your left leg as high as possible, now lift the right leg to join it. Hold and slowly lower them together. Repeat six times each side.

2. In the same position, this time lift your right leg up and down six times. Roll over and repeat with the other leg.

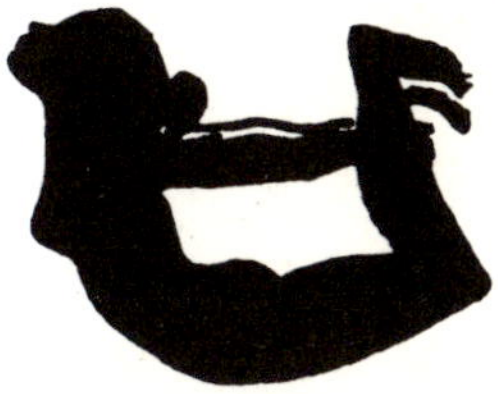

3. Now lying on your stomach, with your arms stretched out in front, lift your arms and legs, then catch hold of your ankles and rock backwards and forwards.

One day an Italian client looked at me and said 'you are hippy today'. For a moment I thought she meant my clothes but unfortunately not: she'd meant my hips. But she offered a solution and here it is:

4. Lie on the floor, bring your knees up to the chest and clasp them there with your right arm. Now roll backwards and forwards, up and down on your left hip twenty times, then twenty

times on your right side. This is quite an effort and might produce bruising: but after a week your hips, waist and even upper thighs will have been whittled away.

Back

These exercises will not only strengthen but slim down your back.

1. Take a chair and rest your hands on the back of it, your body in a bent position and your head up. Drop the head, and raise it again as slowly as possible. Repeat this exercise ten times.

2. Lie on your stomach and hold a heavy book behind your head. Now try lifting your head and shoulders, keeping your hips and feet on the ground. Hold for six seconds, then relax slowly to a count of six. Repeat several times.

3. Lie on your back, lift both legs together, keeping your knees straight, and try to touch the floor behind your head. Go back to starting position, lowering your legs as slowly as possible.

Bottom

This, like the stomach, is another classic problem area.

1. Lie face downwards on your stomach with your chin resting on your hands. Lift one leg at a time, keeping your hips on the ground, your leg straight, and without moving the rest of your body. Repeat this five times with each leg.

2. Again lying on your stomach, but this time with knees bent and supporting yourself on your elbows. Lift right knee off the floor and lower it slowly. Repeat with the left leg. Remember to keep your hips on the floor.

3. In the same position, lift both legs together and also your shoulders, so that you are in a curved position. Hold for six seconds.

4. Sit on the floor with your legs stretched out in front of you and your knees and back straight. Now walk on your bottom, forwards and backwards for as long as you can – a marching record, to accompany you, will keep you going.

5. Wherever you are, sitting in the office or cinema, or waiting in a bus queue, try pulling in your buttocks and abdomen. Pull them in really tightly, hold, then relax. Repeat this at least ten times. An American woman I met has actually trained herself to

walk around with her buttocks always pulled in like this – so now she has a small pert upright bottom.

Legs

Almost everyone feels that their legs could be slightly improved. Exercise and massage are really the only ways in which to bring about any sort of change. I give you some hints on massage later, but now we concentrate on exercise.

the whole leg Stand with your feet parallel and arms relaxed in front. Bend your knees keeping your heels on the ground, repeat three times and on the third bend raise your heels and go right down on the ground. Rise slowly to a count of four, five and six, stretching your arms above your head. Repeat *four* times.

thighs 1. A well-known exercise which produces good results is to lie on the floor with your arms outstretched. Pull your knees up, keeping your feet flat on the ground, and swing your knees from side to side, bumping your thighs hard on the floor. This helps the hips too.

2. Still lying on the floor but with the legs stretched out and arms at shoulder level, bend your left leg so that the knee touches the chest, swing it high into the air and over and across to touch your outstretched right hand back to starting position, then down. Repeat with your right leg. Do it alternately, at least twelve times.

3. Stand with your legs wide apart, imagining a line down the centre of your body. Keeping your back straight and your legs well pulled up, sway your hips from side to side. You can feel the inner thigh working. What could be easier – and it works!

calves and ankles 1. Stand with your heels on the floor and your toes resting on a large, thick book. Lift yourself on to your toes, hold for a count of ten, and then lower yourself slowly. Repeat several times.

2. This is good for the knees as well. Either standing or lying with your legs together and arms relaxed, raise your left leg, point your toe and stiffen your knee and draw circles in the air with your toes. First clockwise then anti-clockwise four times each way. Repeat with the right foot.

depilatories These are not strictly anything to do with the exercizing of your legs but certainly help with their general appearance. Hair on the legs in many countries isn't thought of as being unattractive as it generally is here: but Western women do tend to 'de-fuzz' as a regular part of their beauty routine.

The simplest way is to shave. The strongest criticism of this method is that one has to shave very regularly or end up with legs like cactus plants. Creaming is virtually the same as shaving: a superficial cutting of the hairs. Waxing pulls out the hair from the root, so it has a more lasting effect, from three to four weeks. When the hairs do grow again they are not bristly, and this method usually does, eventually, weaken and diminish the growth. The most effective method is by electrolysis at a beauty salon. This, however, is a mammoth job, slow and expensive. (I even know several women who *pluck* out all the hairs from their legs – this must require enormous reserves of time and patience!)

Of course, the best thing of all, unless it's absolutely necessary, is to do nothing. I always curse the day I started to shave my legs: the hair was quite fine and now it's a continual problem.

But if you do want to be 'hairless', try this wax, the recipe for which an Indian friend in Kenya gave me.

500g (1 lb 2 oz) sugar
Juice of 2 lemons

1½ teaspoons glycerine

Melt the sugar in the lemon juice and simmer very slowly until golden brown, cook for 10 minutes and then remove from the heat. Add the glycerine, mix and use as warm as possible. Using a wooden spoon or a spatula, apply the wax downwards in thin strips to the leg; press it down and then put a piece of cloth on top. Again press, and pull the cloth off towards you, bringing with it the wax and hair.

Before applying it to your legs always test it for heat by applying a little on the inside of the wrist; for if you use the wax too hot it will burn your legs. For cloths, I use strips of an old sheet but anything similar will do. For the wax to be effective you must let the hairs be fairly long before using it, so that there is something for the wax to stick to.

When my friend uses this wax it is simple, quick and marvellously effective. The first time I tried it I got into a fearful mess, but practice makes perfect and it does work, and takes the hairs out from the roots.

Feet

'What a beautiful bird you are with your glorious tail and diadem of gorgeous feathers,' they said. 'But,' cried the Peacock, 'look at my ugly feet.' (Saadi)

We should never allow this to be true of our feet but, somehow they always seem to be forgotten. Although the hardest-working part of the body, our feet get nothing like the attention and pampering that they deserve. We all know that if our feet are aching it is impossible to look, or feel, relaxed. You only have to look at people in the street to verify this – you can always tell the women whose feet are killing her, by the pained expression on her face.

Feet contain about a quarter of all the bones in the body, and Leonardo da Vinci referred to the foot as 'the greatest engineering device in the world'. It is up to us to keep it that way. First check your shoes, as vanity can go too far sometimes: corns, callouses and bunions are generally caused by excess pressures from ill-fitting shoes; heels that are too high throw the weight of the body off balance, onto the metatarsals, causing backache and strain. If you do have any complaint go to the chiropodist immediately, because the longer you leave it, the worse it will get.

Rough skin can easily be removed at home by rubbing with a pumice stone. Remember to give your feet a pedicure and to cream them. In Italy the women seem to take more care of their feet and their beautifully pedicured toes make them look so pampered. As Shakespeare said, 'There's language in her eye, her cheek, her lip, Nay her foot speaks.'

foot massage It is extremely relaxing to have your feet massaged. In fact, the Chinese believe you can relieve all tension, and even cure diseases, by simply massaging and manipulating the feet.

After your bath, when your foot is relaxed, pull and do rotary movements on each toe. Then, with both hands, stroke and knead both the top and the sole of the foot, always moving towards the ankle. It's rather awkward reaching your own feet and is obviously much easier to massage someone else's. Maybe you can arrange to swop foot massages with a friend. At first it will seem strange, and you will probably be convulsed with laughter, but once you realize that it doesn't necessarily tickle, and you master how to do it, you will be amazed at how relaxing it is. You will also improve the circulation and relieve swollen feet.

I have been told, by women of various nationalities, that period pains can be alleviated by massage behind the ankle, all around the achilles tendon. This relieves that nagging back-ache almost immediately, and is really worth trying.

tired and aching feet Tired feet can be refreshed by giving them a

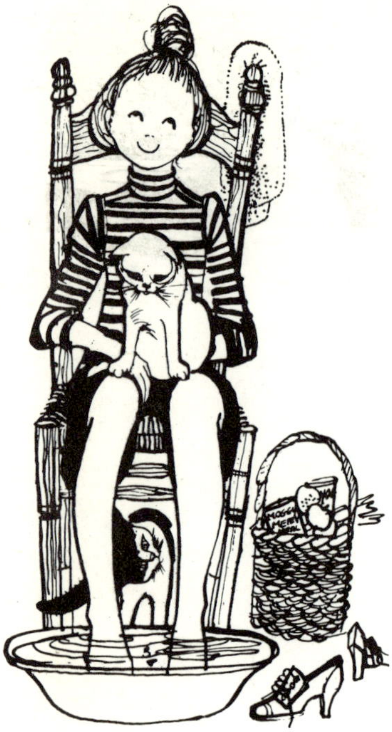

reviving foot bath. Fill a bowl with warm water, add a tablespoon of ordinary washing soda and a handful of herbs – mint, yarrow, lavender, camomile or rosemary. Now soak your feet in this soothing water until you feel revitalized. The smell alone should help. Lavender oil added to a foot bath is supposed to be particularly restorative.

Another soothing water for the feet is to mix one tablespoon of borax and a tablespoon of epsom salts in a bowl of hot water. Or simply use plain salt water which is most refreshing. Alum powder sprinkled on the feet is very good when they are tired and sore. It also hardens them up extraordinarily well.

Nettles are also good for aching feet. Pick a handful – remembering to wear gloves – and put them in a bowl of hot water. When the water has cooled slightly put your feet in and relax. Nettles have 'drawing' properties and this is most effective for refreshing tired feet.

The best way, perhaps, to revive tired feet is simply to 'put them up'. Lie down with your feet higher than your head, either on a pillow or against the wall. This not only relieves the feet, but also the legs. If you suffer from aching veins you should do this for ten minutes at least twice a day to help the circulation and relieve the pressure.

foot exercises 1. A simple one to relax tense feet is to stand with your feet flat on the floor and curl your toes under as tightly as possible, relax and repeat several times.

2. To strengthen your toes, stand with your feet apart and hands at the top of the legs. Bend your right knee and put all your weight on the ball of the right foot, bounce four times and then repeat with the left leg. This exercise should separate your toes.

3. If you like doing your exercises in comfort, sit down and roll a milk-bottle backwards and forwards using first one foot and then the other. Of course, if you're feeling madly ambitious, you might try two bottles at the same time.

4. Picking things up with your toes strengthens the feet – and saves bending down!

To relax tension

Living at the pace we do, each of us is bound to feel tense occasionally. Being able to release that tension, to relax completely, is one of the most important beauty secrets. Tension can all too often be the cause of skin complaints ranging from excessive greasiness and blushing, to eczema and hair loss. So, as you sit reading this, do a relaxing exercise. Drop your head down and let your arms, shoulders, and hands fall limply. Relax completely and go to pieces like a rag doll. Stay like that for a minute.

Now read on. Most people don't *know* how to relax properly, or at least are uncertain about how to start, so here are a couple of other methods.

The ancient relaxation exercise called *Takhfif* – 'the lightness' – which I learned in Turkey, was for many centuries a closely-guarded secret of the imperial Ottomans. It has a wonderfully lightening effect. Lie down and direct your thoughts to your limbs, starting with the right foot. Relax your toes and foot, imagine that they are weightless. Then repeat the same process of relaxation with your right leg, the right side of the body and up to the shoulder. Then do the same with your right hand, fingers first, and again up to the shoulder, neck and head. Repeat in the same manner up the left side. Then imagine that there is a soft current of ease and relaxation passing through your whole body, in the same succession, smoothly and continuously.

Another method is to lie warmly covered in a darkened room with your feet higher than your head. Close your eyes and slowly tense or tighten every part of your body until everything is rigid, and hold as long as possible. Then suddenly let go and relax. Repeat this several times, then rest in this relaxed position trying to keep your mind a blank.

the 'laying on of leaves' In my search for cosmetic recipes I have often come across references to the 'laying on of leaves'. The basic idea is to bind leaves to the body, and the juices from the leaves are said to have dramatic effects on the health of the patient. An old English recipe (in *Queen's Closet Opened*, 1668) advocates: 'For sore eyes that come from hot tumours, take elder leaves and chafe them between the hands and lay them on the nape of the neck.' And an Afghan manuscript states: 'Grape leaves bound for one hour with bandages on the limbs increase vivacity in the indolent. Fig leaves, applied in the same manner, reduce nervousness and temperament.' I thought this latter such a crazy idea that I tried applying fresh grape leaves to my legs, and found that I felt extremely energetic. Whether this was the action of the leaves, or purely psychological, I don't know, but *something* happened! (It could have been because of the enzymes in the juices.) And the laying on of leaves is certainly not limited to old manuscripts and incorrigible experimenters like myself: I recently came across a

newspaper report from Japan bearing a picture of a woman receiving treatment in a very modern beauty salon, who was completely bound up in leaves.

Anyway it is a lovely crazy idea and always worth trying if only to amuse yourself!

Massage

Massage makes one feel pampered, which I think we all need. It is one of the best ways of relieving tension and making one relax, both of which are vitally important in the hectic world we live in. It stimulates the blood, nourishes, smoothes, tones and softens the skin. It can even, if practised strenuously enough, maintain muscle tone, and this stimulation makes one feel thinner, more lithe, and generally more cared for, healthier and happier.

In eastern countries it is totally accepted that both men and women have massage, and everyone knows the rudiments of how to do it. Here in the West we have lost the art. Many people here are reserved about massage which I think is partly due to our puritanical background – 'if it is too enjoyable and pleasurable it must be wrong'! But massage can relieve tension – and how much healthier to have a massage than a tranquillizing pill. We all ought to learn how to massage each others' backs, shoulders and necks; it is such a simple effective way of relieving aches and pains. Simply stroke the back and see how this can relieve the pressure. Next time someone has a headache, or your husband comes in exhausted from work, try massaging his back. Just stroke the shoulders and neck, then do rotary and kneading movements on his shoulders. Ask him to do the same for you next time you are tired,.so that he learns too! And occasionally treat yourself to a professional massage to be thoroughly pampered.

Be your own masseuse

Now for the less relaxing type of massage: the massage that breaks down the fat. Few of us can afford the time or money to have a regular professional massage, so here is how to do it yourself. The treatment is obviously not going to be relaxing, but hard and stimulating instead. It will increase the circulation, leaving your body feeling alive and invigorated (and if you suffer from *bad* circulation – if your fingers and toes ever feel numb – massage will alleviate this). You can also soothe and ease tense muscles.

If you are feeling flabby, regular self-massage can contribute towards getting rid of those bulges, and smoothe out that unsightly 'bobbly' fat which so often appears when you have put on weight – and which is so often mistaken for cellulite. In fact, wherever you have a pad of fat – massage it.

The basic movements of self-massage are stroking, kneading, wringing, pinching, rolling and clapping.

stroking This is exactly what the name implies, and its primary purpose is to apply oil to the area to be massaged. The hands should be easy and relaxed, and you just stroke up the limb towards the heart. The movement, when done gently, soothes and relaxes the muscles and nerves. When done firmly, it can stimulate the blood flow.

kneading This is also known as *petrissage*. Pretend you are kneading bread – pick up the flesh and squeeze it. Use the whole hand, holding the fingers loosely together, and press the fat with the palm of the hands: pick up and press. It is almost like pinching, but is a much larger movement.

pinching The same as kneading but using only the thumb and forefingers.

wringing You work with both hands. Imagine you are wringing out a cloth. Pick up the fat and squeeze and twist it. Practise on your thighs and most of us have extra flesh there, and it's easy to get at.

rolling With your hands facing each other pick up about an inch of flesh. With pressure from your thumb, press and roll the flesh over the surface. This is especially good for breaking down 'bobbly' fat.

clapping and slapping Again this is just what the name implies. Slap yourself with flat hands, cupped hands, the edge of hands with the fingers held loose, the back of the hands and even with your fists – in fact any way you can, and the more variety the better. It is a rhythmic, fast, bouncy movement which stimulates the flow of the blood to the skin. Avoid doing it on any area where you have broken veins.

All these movements may seem awkward at first, but with practice they will become easy. Do the movements either in the bath – the water stops it from hurting – or after the bath when the body is relaxed. It is marvellous for the thighs, all over the tummy or diaphragm, and that other forgotten area – the upper arms. For your massage use either one of your scented oils or the creams on p. 132 .

By massaging yourself you will become more aware of your body – especially when dieting, which changes one's whole mental attitude – and will help you to *feel* and *look* slimmer.

legs 1. Stroke up the calf and up to the top of the thigh.

2. Knead the calf muscle which can easily become very tense. This kneading movement is large and firm.

3. Fat often accumulates around the knee, and so pinch and stroke all around that area.

thighs The thighs are easy to massage, and most of us would benefit from a bit of attention there.

1. Deep stroke the whole area.

2. Wring, knead and squeeze the whole area with a hard, fast, rhythmic movement. Try doing it to music – the beat makes the movement easier to maintain.

3. Keep your wrist supple and 'slap' with a hard, bouncy movement.

feet Massaging your feet is incredibly relaxing, and the next time you feel really tired or tense, do try it.
If you sit cross-legged on the floor, or on a chair with your ankle resting on your knee, you can easily reach and massage your foot.

1. Stroke the whole foot.

2: Make large rotary movements all around the instep and under the toes using either the forefingers or thumbs.

3. Small rotary pressures. Press, rotate, release, move on; press, rotate, release.

bottom and hips Massage of the hips is very similar to that of the thighs.

1. Deep stroke in semi-circles up from the thighs to the hips.

2. Knead and wring every area of the bottom and hips that you can reach.

stomach 1. Stroke the tummy with large circular movements using the whole hand.

2. Using both hands make rotary kneading movements around the lower stomach.

3. Squeeze and pinch the fat on the diaphragm using the thumb and forefinger.

arms 1. Stroke up the arm from the hand to the shoulder.

2. Knead around the joints, the fingers, wrists and elbows.

3. Knead and pinch the bicep muscle on the upper arm. Pay attention also to the back of the arm where fat tends to accumulate. The circulation is also bad there, causing little spots; massage and scrubbing can alleviate this.

shoulders and neck 1. Stroke and knead the shoulder using the opposite hand.

2. Using the fingertips, do firm, rotary pressure movements around the shoulder-blade, then in towards the spine, and up the neck to the scalp.

3. Stroke firmly around the base of the neck.

back The only part that is really accessible is the base of the spine. Massage here can be very relaxing and can alleviate backaches.

1. Do deep rotary movements starting from the base of the spine and going as high as you can reach. Do the rotations on either side of the spine using the fingertips, resting the whole hand lightly on the back.

2. Again do deep rotary movements around the middle back, using either the thumbs or the knuckles. This is beautifully relaxing and eases any tautness of the muscles.

Slimming

I am not going to go into any detail about the slimming process itself, or diets. The basic principles of diet – what is good for you, what is bad, and what is fattening – are well enough known that I don't need to repeat them here. And, anyway, newspapers and magazines deal with individual diets quite frequently, and I'm sure that the majority of them, if followed stringently, would be effective. Most of you will know the particular diet that suits you, and if you follow the instructions and hints throughout this book – eating good, natural foods such as lean meat, fresh vegetables and fruit, drinking lots of water; exercizing and massaging with the occasional one-day fast – you should not have too many problems.

Slimming aids

But there are a number of traditional or amusing ways of helping along the slimming process, and I list them below.

fennel In almost every old herbal book I have read there has been a reference to fennel for slimming. For instance from *The Good Housekeeper*, 1596, 'To make one slender, take fennel and seeth it in water, a very good quantity, and wringing out the juice thereof when it is mixed, drink it first and last, and it shall swage either man or woman.'

So next time you go on a diet why not try it? Make a strong

infusion of fennel and drink it instead of tea. Chewing fresh fennel leaves also helps to reduce the appetite.

elm leaves These are used similarly, and a farmer told me that in his youth they used to chew elm leaves when they were harvesting and hadn't time to go home and eat.

dandelions These are also known for their slimming and diuretic properties (the latter has led to dandelions being known as 'piss en lit', and many other, less restrained, local names). Make a strong infusion and drink it twice a day.

potato juice While on a diet one can often become constipated, and recently a woman told me that potato juice was a miraculous cure for this. She drinks a wine glass of the juice each morning (no more, as it is so powerful) and says it is the only thing that has ever helped her. (Unfortunately, the only way I know to obtain this is by using a juice extractor, which not everyone owns – I don't.)

snow and ice A Georgian woman told me that this tones the body wonderfully. Apply when possible to opposite side of the arms, legs and body at the same time. These ice packs help the slimming process, especially if applied to the non-fat parts of the body at each treatment.

Try this on a hot summer's day, when we tried it we had fits of laughter. I think it probably works by making the tiny muscles contract and thus toning the whole body.

'A lady of beauty and elegant form needs neither ornaments nor precious rings.'

Saadi

HANDS

Hands are always in evidence and however well-groomed or beautiful a woman may be, the illusion is shattered if her hands are uncared for. Rough, chapped, wrinkled hands are not always the result of either age or hard work; they could be lined and rough at twenty and soft and unlined at eighty. Their condition depends on the care you take of them. Detergents and soap and water constantly dry the skin, so try, try, *try* to wear rubber gloves when doing housework or washing up. (In fact, ideally, you should cover your hands with cream, then put on cotton gloves, and *then* the rubber gloves. In that way you are not only protecting your hands but giving them a treatment at the same time.) I am afraid that I am one of those people who finds it just impossible to do anything with my gloves on – I am always buying them but never actually get round to using them. Instead I have to try and repair the damage, and I am constantly rubbing cream into my hands. Keep a pot of cream next to the basin and apply some after you wash. Massaging the cream in helps stimulate the circulation, thus feeding the skin.

A very simple barrier cream can be made by mixing 1 cup rosewater, half a cup of glycerine and 2 tablespoons lemon juice (use a commercial pure juice as this lasts longer than fresh lemon juice, which tends to grow a mould). Lemons are a great asset to your hands, softening, cleaning and bleaching them. (Never throw a squeezed half lemon away, but use it instead to rub and clean your hands and elbows.)

If, however, you have got your hands into bad condition through too much gardening or housework, coat them with a really rich cream and then wear cotton gloves. The heat will help the hands absorb the cream (lanolin, strongly advocated by Marlene Dietrich, is beautifully rich and ideal for this treatment). For centuries, women have worn these gloves to bed in order to

restore work-stained hands and whiten the skin: in Elizabethan England, court ladies would sleep with their hands coated in cream, wearing perfumed bed gloves – the pomades being especially scented with musk, civet and ambergris to perfume and whiten the hands; while in France, the women would use a white lead ointment containing melon and mustard seeds and bitter almonds which was considered most effective for whitening but highly poisonous! But – and do please, take note – the moisture of some of these pomades could just cause some rheumatic discomfort.

'*an excellent preparation for your sleeping gloves:* Hands that are inclined to chap should be rubbed over frequently with a paste of one spoonful of honey and two of fine oatmeal. Beat these up with the yolks of two eggs and add sufficient unsalted lard to make a paste; thoroughly mix all together. This preparation will be found excellent for smearing your sleeping gloves with' (*Aids to Health and Beauty*, 1898).

protective hand paste One recipe for a protective hand cream was given to me by an Austrian woman who has lovely soft hands and she swears by this cream. She puts it on before working and then rinses it off when she has finished.

Mix together into a paste (it makes too much for one day's use so put the rest in a screw-topped jar, for it will harden if the air gets to it) and use it whenever possible. Surprisingly this paste is not at all greasy, and I also use it on my knees, elbows and feet, all of which can always do with extra attention.

1 egg yolk
2 teaspoons kaolin
1 teaspoon almond or safflower oil

hand mask Yes, I did say hand mask.

Mix to a paste and apply this to your hands for about ten minutes. It leaves them beautifully soft. It can of course be used with your 'bed gloves'.

1½ tablespoons oatmeal
1 tablespoon warm water
1 teaspoon olive oil
1 teaspoon lemon juice
1 teaspoon glycerine

almond hand cream Melt together the oils and waxes, remove from the heat and then slowly add the separately heated water in which you have dissolved the borax. Just stir manually for this cream – don't worry, it sets quickly! In fact the moment you add the water the cream turns a beautiful pure white. These quantities make about half a cup of marvellous soft cream which I perfume by adding almond essence but you could use anything

2 teaspoons lanolin
1½ teaspoons cocoa butter
1 tablespoon beeswax
5 teaspoons light liquid paraffin
1 teaspoon almond oil

2 tablespoons water
¼ teaspoon borax

Perfume: almond essence

you happen to have – lavender oil, thyme or perhaps even peach extract which makes a very luxurious cream. This is my favourite hand cream, because it really isn't greasy, so there is no excuse not to use it always after washing your hands.

2 tablespoons glycerine
2 tablespoons cornflour

1 cup orange-flower water (or rosewater)

simple hand cream Heat the glycerine and gradually add the cornflour to make a thick paste. Slowly mix in the orange-flower water and stir until it thickens. This hand cream is very inexpensive and just a good as any commercial product. Pour into labelled jars – and use.

In France, during the sixteenth century, women cleansed their hands with orange-flower water, made in Italian convents, believing that it possessed special protective virtues against contagious diseases.

1 tablespoon stearic acid
2 teaspoons almond oil
1 teaspoon emulsifying wax

6 tablespoons water
1 tablespoon glycerine
¼ teaspoon detergent

satin hand cream Melt the oils and heat the waters in separate bowls as usual. Remove from the heat and slowly add the water to the oil, beating all the time with your electric beater on low speed. The cream turns white immediately and within a couple of minutes you will have about half a cup of pure white, satiny cream which soaks in instantly leaving a pearly sheen to your hands. I find this cream so effective that I also use it as a body lotion. The recipe was given to me by a beautiful Caucasian woman who, though well into her sixties, had the hands of a young girl. And, as you know, it is hands which show the first signs of age.

russian hand cleanser A Russian princess told me that sugar and oil rubbed together in the hands after heavy toil instantly turns them into a lady's hands again!

Hand massage and exercises

These both help the circulation and you will be surprised to find how they alleviate tension and stiffness.

Always massage towards the wrist using the thumb and index finger. Start with the little finger making small rotary movements on each joint, then rotate and pull the whole finger. When you have done this to each finger, massage from the knuckles to the wrist in the same way: using the thumb, you press and rotate in between the knuckles gradually working down to the wrist.

1. Stretch your fingers out as tautly as possible, relax and then throw them out again. Repeat this several times and you will feel all your muscles working.

2. Shake your hands until they are completely relaxed and limp.

3. Circle your hands from the wrist, making the circle as deep as possible and doing four circles to the right and then four to the left. Repeat several times.

Nails

Nails are made of a horny substance known as keratin, the same as the hair and, like hair again, the nail we see is dead. The nail plate or growing area is several millimetres below the base of the nail, and it takes about nine months for a new nail to grow. Healthy nails need a healthy diet containing a lot of protein – vegetables, fruit, meat, fish, eggs etc. – and Vitamin B, which is found in yeast, bread and oatmeal.

Cuticle care

The quickest way of ruining the nails is to have rough manicures and to use metal instruments. Never, ever, cut the cuticle, or press it down with a steel instrument, instead massage it with cuticle cream and press the cuticle down with a hoof stick (a wooden orangestick with a rubber pad at the end). Although beauty shops sell cuticle scissors, they should not be used (except by a skilled operator) as they are highly damaging to the nail and harden the skin of the cuticle. As a child I was taught when drying my hands I should gently push back the cuticles with the towel. This is easy to do and does help keep the cuticles in good shape.

The only way we can help the growth of the nail is by massaging the cuticle and the area just below which brings the blood to the surface and feeds the growing nail.

lanolin cuticle cream Nails contain cholesterin which is a constituent of lanolin, so this makes an excellent cuticle cream. Either use pure lanolin or mix a little kaolin into it to make a paste.

2 tablespoons lanolin
2 teaspoons kaolin (or powdered lecithin)

cuticle cream Mix 2 tablespoons of pure petroleum jelly with a half teaspoon glycerine and a drop of red food colouring (cochineal), and beat them together. You will be amazed to find that you have made a perfect cuticle cream identical to many which are on the market.

Buffing

In my opinion the most beautiful hands are those with well-manicured, natural, shiny nails. Unfortunately to achieve this 'natural look' takes a tremendous amount of care. The hands and nails have to be immaculately clean and smooth, and the nails well-shaped and pearly. One way to achieve this, apart from constant application of cream, is to use a buffer. A buffer is a little pad covered in chamois leather and you polish the unvarnished nail with it; this stimulates the circulation and strengthens the nails as well as making them shiny. In Victorian and Edwardian days every woman had a chamois leather buffer on her dressing table and it was her maid's duty to see that there was a fresh piece of leather on it each day. I am glad to see that we no longer need to search for them in antique shops for they are now available in many chemists' shops again.

Bleaching

If you smoke, or often wear nail varnish, you'll sometimes notice that your nails become discoloured. If this is the case, try this nail-bleaching recipe.

3 tablespoons orange-flower water
1 teaspoon lemon juice (either fresh or pure bottled)

lemon bleach Mix these together in a bottle and apply as often as possible.

A French manicurist told me to simply use plain lemon juice. She squeezes a lemon and puts the juice into an old empty nail varnish bottle, then with the brush already in the bottle paints her nails with it at least twice a day. She said that it not only bleaches the nails but also strengthens them. A Greek client of mine tried it after her pregnancy when her nails constantly broke and was thrilled with the results; in fact she says they have *never* been so good.

1 tablespoon glycerine
4 tablespoons hydrogen peroxide (5 vol.)
5 tablespoons rosewater

for smokers Mix all ingredients together and apply as often as necessary – this will bleach those nicotine stains from the fingers and nails.

Removing nail varnish

The most harmful part of wearing nail varnish is its removal, as varnish removers strip the nail of oil leaving them brittle. So try this. Buy a bottle of Acetone from the chemist and add a teaspoon of glycerine to it – this stops it from being too drying. and is much cheaper than buying a proprietary brand.

Strengthening

An American dermatologist told me that the commonest cause of soft, breaking nails is not diet but detergents and household cleaners. He also mentioned that calcium, although renowned for building the nails, did not seem particularly helpful; but that gelatine was. In an experiment carried out in a New York hospital both patients and nurses took a daily dose of 1 tablespoon of unflavoured gelatine. Marked improvements in their nails were noticed after as little as two or three months.

Two to three kelp tablets taken daily also strengthen the nails.

iris flowers Culpepper declares that blue iris flowers steeped in water overnight and brushed regularly on the nails will greatly strengthen them.

elm leaves A Kashmiri recipe recommends using an infusion of elm leaves. Steep clean nails in this preparation every day for three weeks, and this will prevent brittleness.

Nail colourings

In Egypt, during the reign of the Pharoahs, the woman of noble birth had their nails rubbed with golden ointment containing henna. This coloured their nails so that they contrasted with their pale complexions, showing that they did no manual work.

Henna is still used for colouring the nails all over the East. One Moroccan friend buffs her nails first and then colours them with henna, which gives them a soft natural reddish-brown tint. Mix 2 tablespoons of henna with the juice of a lemon and enough hot tea to make a paste. Paint this on to the nails with a paint brush and leave it on for ten to twenty minutes depending on the depth of colour you want.

In fact while you are colouring your nails you might try painting your hands with henna. All over Morocco you see women with the most delicate intricate designs painted in henna on the palms of their hands (and, incidentally, the soles of their feet). Mix the henna (about 2 tablespoons), lemon juice and tea with a clove of crushed garlic – which fixes it – and with a stick draw a design. Needless to say it is infinitely easier to do it on someone else, and I think it looks marvellous. One word of warning though, it does stain the hand and so you will not be able to wash it off. It wears off naturally in a few weeks.

In China they used to colour their nails with a vegetable dye. A plant known as 'Finger Nail Plant' produces a red sap and this, when painted on, makes the nails a beautiful red. Once again this cannot be taken off and has to be grown out. A Chinese friend of mine was fascinated by this as a child, and remembers getting her nurse to cut her nails and seeing that the colour went all the way through the cross section.

'First time he kissed me, he but only kissed
The fingers of this hand wherewith I write;
And, ever since, it grew more clean and white.'
Elizabeth Barratt Browning

THE SUN AND YOUR SKIN

Whether or not you have a sun tan is dictated by fashion. In Victorian times and before, women went to extraordinary lengths to stay out of the sun; the paler their skin the greater their beauty. Nowadays we want the opposite – the browner the better – and we seem to be obsessed with being suntanned. We think of a tan being almost synonymous with health – but we are wrong. Unfortunately, there is ever-increasing evidence to show that the sun is destructive to skin, and one dermatologist has gone as far as to say that the worst thing we could *do* for our skin is to expose it to the sun. The sun's action on the skin is exactly the same as that of age: it dehydrates leaving the skin thick, leathery, wrinkled and dry; it also causes broken veins, freckles and brown patches. So beware of too much sun (although in moderation it is good for you in that the vitamin D created by sunlight is necessary for healthy bones).

One answer is that, instead of roasting for hours in the sun, you should try using a false tan. These creams and lotions are simple to use and if you are careful over the knees, elbows and ankles, will give a lovely natural tan. I know lots of people who never sunbathe but always look brown because they use these lotions which are especially useful before going on holiday. Appearing on a beach lily-white can be embarrassing. These will also prevent you from trying to get brown too quickly – and ending up burnt.

Suntan lotions and creams

But if, like most of us, you worship the sun and crave to be brown, here are some ideas and suggestions to help along a more effective – and safer – tan. Firstly, in the sun and on the beach, it is essential to protect the skin as much as possible. In hot areas all over the world, there are very many different ways of protecting the skin while tanning it. In Morocco I was told to use tomato juice; in Cannes a mixture of oil and bergamot; in Spain a mixture of sunflower oil and pure lemon juice; and in Italy an old woman said the best thing to use was sea weed, which you simply rub all over your skin, the iodine in it helping to give you a safe tan.

But whatever you use, use plenty, be really lavish. One of the oldest and best-known oils is the following.

1 cup olive or sesame oil
½ cup vinegar
1 teaspoon iodine

oil and vinegar This 'salad dressing' suntan cream is easy to make and very effective – and if you don't want to smell too like a salad, add a few drops of perfume (lavender oil is good as it also helps to keep insects away).

super-suntan cream I was happily using oil and vinegar until a friend came back from a week's holiday in Hawaii with a beautiful tan three times darker than mine, and her skin was still smooth and soft. Here is the recipe she learned there:

4 tablespoons lanolin
3 tablespoons sesame oil
2 tablespoons almond oil

½ cup very strong tea

Make the tea twenty minutes before mixing the oils, using four tea bags and squeezing them occasionally to make the tea very strong. Melt the oils in an enamel bowl over a water bath. Remove from the heat, add the strained tea, and beat either with a wooden spoon or an electric beater on low speed. Perfume it with a few drops of fresh smelling essential oil – lemon grasse, lavender, or one of your home-made herb oils. Now you have about a cup of lovely soft fluffy cream.

The lanolin and almond oil in this recipe feed the skin, keeping it soft and moist. The sesame oil is a polyunsaturated oil and the one which most fully absorbs the ultra-violet rays of the sun. The tea is used because the tannin also absorbs the sun's burning rays, making it a mild sunscreen, and is soothing to the skin (it's frequently used to take the sting out of burns).

This cream enables you to tan fairly fast, and is good for nearly every skin type except the very fair and sensitive skin. If you have this skin type, this cream isn't protective enough for you at first,

and you will need one of the modern sun screeners. You can use this when you are more used to the sun and already have a slight tan.

sesame seed lotion Grind the sesame seeds in a coffee grinder then add them to the rosewater in a pint bottle and *shake* vigorously. Let it stand for a day, shaking as often as possible. Strain and add the vodka or spirit to preserve it. This lotion uses sesame seeds instead of the sesame oil, but still possesses the same basic properties as it will absorb the ultra-violet rays, and you will tan quite quickly.

4 tablespoons sesame seeds
1 cup rosewater
4 tablespoons vodka (or, if you can bear the smell, surgical spirit)

bergamot oil All over the continent, especially in the South of France, the most popular suntanning lotion is a mixture of coconut oil and bergamot oil. This combination gives you an amazingly fast tan and has a fantastic smell.

Melt the coconut oil (it melts very easily) and add the bergamot oil. *Never* use more than three per cent bergamot oil to coconut oil, because if it is used any stronger it can cause the sun to burn the skin and produce brown patches. While still liquid, though cooled, pour the mixture into a plastic bottle ready for use on the beach. Coconut oil sets when it is cold thus becoming non-spillable, and very useful for travelling.

1 cup coconut oil (or olive oil)
¼ teaspoon bergamot oil

On holiday still scrub your body. Don't be scared of scrubbing all your tan off. By rubbing you get rid of the dead skin so you will just be removing skin that would otherwise peel off anyway. If your skin is smooth and soft it will not flake and peel so your tan will last better.

Sunburnt?

Even when we are careful we can still sometimes get sunburnt. Don't forget that you can be burned by the reflected heat from water, snow or sand and so, even if you're in the shade, or wearing a hat, do still use a sun-screen cream. If you are burned badly go to a doctor, but if you are just lobster red and sore, here are some cooling, soothing suggestions.

gin Apply it neat using a piece of damp cotton wool and it will soothe the skin and stop the stinging.

lettuce leaves Make an infusion by boiling the outer leaves of a

lettuce for a couple of minutes. The lotion is really soothing. Nettles can be used in the same way.

camomile lotion This is also marvellously cooling when used on a painful red skin. Take a handful of camomile flowers and infuse them in 1 cup of hot water.

tea Ordinary tea (or milk) are common everyday ingredients that will also take the sting out of sunburn.

cucumber Slices rubbed over the painful area are refreshing and so will take some of the heat from the skin.

Pale-skinned beauty (or how to bleach out a fading suntan)
Throughout history women have been trying to bleach their skin. Marie Antoinette used to bathe in buttermilk each day to retain her skin's beautiful pale alabaster colour. You may not tan easily, so why not be different and *cultivate* your pale skin? Make it even whiter by trying these recipes. Or perhaps your suntan has started to fade, leaving your skin with a sallow yellow tinge, so why not bleach it back to its natural colour?

The following old fashioned remedies using lemon, strawberries, limes, milk, buttermilk and yoghourt, not only bleach but also revitalize the skin.

2 tablespoons Fuller's Earth
1 tablespoon witch-hazel
1 teaspoon honey
4 ground cloves

bleaching mask Mix these into a paste, apply and leave on for twenty minutes.

lemon pack Mix one tablespoon Fuller's Earth with one and a half tablespoons lemon or lime juice. This also soothes and tightens the skin.

Afghan bleaching secret Use the whey – clear liquid – from sour milk. This is marvellous for bleaching a discoloured neck as well as an old tan.

bleaching tonic Add half a lemon which has been cut into slices to ½ cup of white wine, boil for a minute and add a teaspoon of castor sugar.

bleaching mask Sieve four strawberries and mix with 1 tablespoon buttermilk.

BATHING

The bath is amazingly versatile: it can be quick and practical for washing only; it can be invigorating and stimulating; it can replace oils and soften the skin; and it can relieve tension and be a complete relaxation.

The cosmetic and therapeutic value of bathing has been known throughout history, and one finds that the most famous beauties had their favourite bath recipe. These include bathing in crushed strawberries, raspberries, wine or champagne – all of which are slightly impractical nowadays, but there are many which we can still easily and usefully adapt.

A multitude of baths

We all know that Cleopatra bathed in asses' milk. So also did Poppaea, the wife of Nero, and when she was exiled from Rome she obtained permission to take forty asses with her to enable her to continue with this luxurious treatment. Nowadays I feel it's unlikely that anyone could, or would use all that milk on one bath, but you can emulate it by simply adding a handful of powdered milk to the bath-water – much simpler, and very nearly as good.

soft-water bath Nell Gwynne always used rainwater in her bath and she managed to keep the love of Charles II. If you cannot get rainwater soften the bath-water by simply adding a little sodium sesqui carbonate.

vinegar bath If you have itchy, dry skin, try adding a cup of vinegar to the bath water. This has been used for centuries and is most effective.

mustard bath If you think you are getting cold, a little mustard powder added to the bath stimulates and heats the skin (keep it to a pinch though, or you'll be bright red).

bran or oatmeal baths Oatmeal and bran contain oils and vegetable hormones which soothe and soften the skin. I use them in conjuction with herb baths to give my skin a thorough treatment. Use one tablespoon of oatmeal in the bath.

honey bath A German doctor recently claimed that if you add a spoonful of honey to your bath, it would relieve tiredness and sleeplessness. When I tried this, it worked beautifully, so I persuaded everyone to try it. We all came to the conclusion that it not only smoothed our jangled nerves, calmed us and made us sleep, but also left our skin feeling smooth and satiny. So even if you never get round to doing anything else in this book, at least try adding a spoonful of honey to your bath. What could be easier?

epsom salts bath Two handfuls added to the bath water relieve tiredness.

a starchy bath A few tablespoons of laundry starch and a teaspoon of glycerine added to the bath water leave your skin feeling beautifully smooth, tight and soft. Because of its tightening effect, this bath can be slightly drying.

herb baths Voltaire described perfumed baths as the 'luxury of luxuries'. Herbs added to the bath are not only highly aromatic but soothing and beneficial to your general health. Don't just throw them in, or you will have to spend hours cleaning out bits of leaf and twig. Make, or buy, draw-string muslin or cheesecloth bags and fill them with herbs, oatmeal or bran. Keep a bag hanging from the bath-tap because in that way you will remember to fill it and use it. Otherwise you'll always *intend* to have a lovely herb bath, but somehow never get around to it. (A friend of mine uses one of those individual tea containers filled with herbs, which is a very good idea.)

The herbs can be used singly, or in mixtures. Lavender, hyssop, mint, pennyroyal, borage, yarrow, rosemary, balm or camomile: in fact, whatever you have in either the kitchen or the garden. Madame de Pompadour and Ninon de Lenclos, two famous French beauties, both always had herb baths, using a mixture of houseleek, mint, lavender, thyme and rosemary. And Catherine the Great is supposed to have been so keen on herbs that she had a special train going from one end of Russia to the other, to get fresh herbs for her cosmetics and herbal baths.

orange bath Oranges were a favourite fruit of an early Chinese Empress, who is said to have bathed in water scented with orange rind. There is an old Chinese poem which, if roughly translated, says: 'What is that sound of galloping hooves and jingling bells on a horse's neck? It is only the royal courier galloping from far away with oranges for the Empress's bath.'

bath salts

These are easily made. Mix two cups of ordinary washing soda with two tablespoons of potassium carbonate and a few drops of an aromatic essential oil – lavender and pine are refreshing. Keep this mixture in a large jar in the bathroom and use about a tablespoon in each bath. Another version is as simple and effective. Mix together 2 cups sodium sesqui carbonate, 2 drops food colouring and 2 teaspoons essential oil, and use.

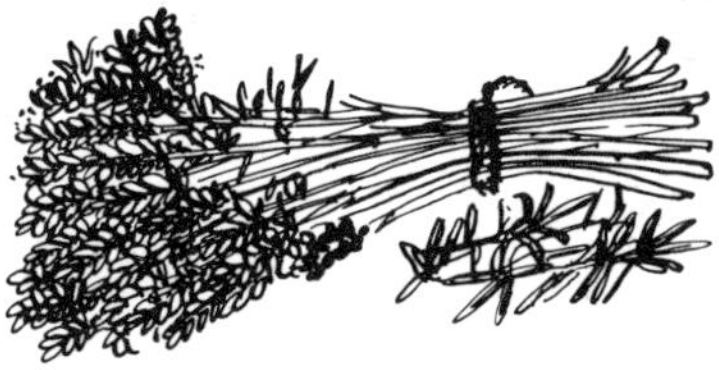

Bath oils

You can simply add any vegetable oil to the bath water: almond, olive or sunflower. Baby or mineral oil is not suitable as it cannot be absorbed by the skin and only rests on the surface. These basic oils can be mixed with some of the herb oils you have made previously, or with any aromatic oil. You will then have a lovely scented bath oil.

2 eggs
¼ cup almond oil
¼ cup sunflower oil (or corn oil)
½ cup safflower oil (or olive)
Optional: 1 teaspoon honey

2 teaspoons washing-up detergent
¼ cup vodka
½ cup milk

Perfume

milk and honey dispersing bath oil So many bath oils just rest on the surface of the water, which means that the only time your skin gets any benefit is when you enter and get out of the water. That is why this bath oil following is so good; it disperses, meaning that it goes into the water, turning it milky, and so the whole time you are lying in the bath your skin is benefitting.

Using the low speed on your electric beater completely blend the eggs and oils together. Now add in the detergent which acts as an emulsifier making it thick. Continue beating and add the vodka – which is the ingredient that makes this bath oil dispersing, and with this minute quantity there is no worry of it drying your skin. Still beating add the milk which will make the oil slightly thinner and very luxurious. Finally, add the perfume: you can use something really exotic. I personally like lemon verbena oil, pine or jasmine oil, but experiment and find the one that you really like. You can add 1 or 2 teaspoons of honey when you have blended the egg and oils. This enriches the oil and makes it even more nourishing and lubricating.

Make this bath oil immediately. It is the best you will ever have used; in fact I am sure you will never be without it. It leaves your skin feeling smooth, satiny, and thoroughly pampered. These quantities should make enough to last you a couple of weeks. Use it quickly as, containing all these fantastic ingredients, it does go off. One word of warning, though, very hot water will inactivate this bath oil, but anyway water that is *too* hot is bad for the skin.

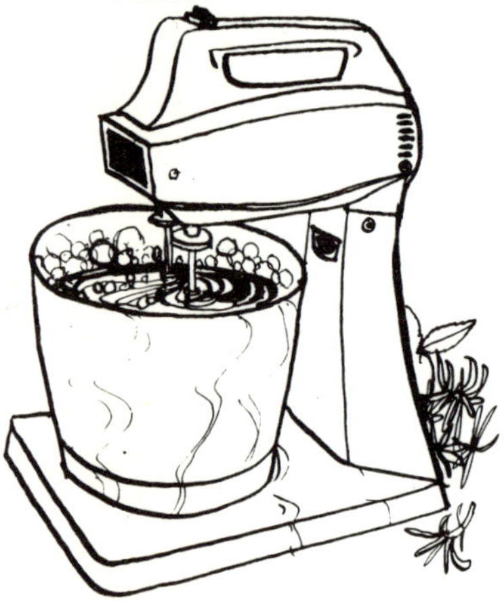

1 egg
½ cup shampoo (cheap and clear)
1 teaspoon gelatine

perfume

bubble bath Mix these together with an electric beater, and add to the bath when the taps are running. The bubbles will start to rise and you will have a luxurious Hollywood-style bubble bath which leaves your skin feeling soft and smooth.

3 tablespoons oatmeal flour
1 tablespoon oatmeal bran
1 tablespoon ground almonds
1 tablespoon wheat flour

perfume

softening bath powder Mix all the ingredients together in a jar. Use only a very little in the bath water each time you bathe. Your skin will benefit tremendously by using this simple recipe.

Body scrubs

I am a great believer in scrubbing the body: it removes dead skin, and improves the circulation, giving the skin a finer texture and better colour. The body is constantly renewing its cells, and whenever we increase the circulation we are aiding this process of replacement.

Before the bath, scrub the whole of your body with a string

glove or loofah. I prefer a string glove as it is stronger and finer. You only need to scrub for a few minutes and your skin will be glowing, and if you remember, or can train yourself to do this every day, you will be amazed at how it will improve your skin. Some people find this method too harsh; if so scrub yourself while in the bath. This is still good, but less abrasive. A Peruvian friend couldn't find a string glove so she used a floor scrubbing brush – but I think this might be taking it a little too far! If you don't have a string glove try scrubbing with sea salt. This is especially effective in getting rid of that grey 'winter skin'. Stand in the bath and rub your body all over with the salt, then rinse it off and oil yourself. Isadora Duncan, the famous American dancer, used to scrub herself with salt each day to keep her skin smooth, supple and elastic.

An Irish woman told me that she uses sugar mixed with oil on her elbows, knees and feet; I tried it on the whole of my body and found it marvellous. The Babylonians rubbed their skin with pumice stone to make it smooth: so this is an old theory which is as useful and beneficial now as it was then.

A Chinese friend of mine told me that her family used to soak in the bath and then with a relatively dry, very well wrung-out flannel, they would rub the skin. Push the flannel firmly upwards, and you find this removes the dead skin at the same time as improving the circulation. You will see dark rolls of dead skin and dirt coming off.

Indian bride's massage secret In India ten days before a girl is to become a bride she is massaged daily with a special powder mixed with jasmine oil. There are seventeen ingredients in this powder and unfortunately most of them are unavailable in this country, so an Indian friend and I use this recipe: The paste thoroughly cleanses and stimulates the skin leaving it soft, shiny and impregnated with the smell of jasmine. In fact in some areas of both India and Pakistan, if you enter a house and it smells strongly of jasmine, you know that a future bride is living there.

1 tablespoon dried, ground and sieved orange peel
1 tablespoon dried, ground and sieved lemon peel
2 tablespoons ground almonds
pinch of salt
4 tablespoons wheatgerm flour
1 tablespoon ground thyme
pinch of ground allspice (optional)
Almond oil (enough to make a workable paste)

Jasmine oil (to perfume)

This idea is so luxurious that I feel we ought to use it ourselves as a special treat. Try to persuade a friend to rub you with it before a really special occasion; and you can massage her some other time. It is really great fun and one feels as though one has gone back in time – like being part of a harem!

Afghan massage paste This consists of a wheat flour or oatmeal mixed into a paste with double cream. The paste has a deep-cleansing effect on the skin, removing dead cells and an amazing amount of dirt. I love the thought that for thousands of years people have been using exactly this treatment. I frequently use it on clients and we are always amazed at how silky it leaves the skin. You can easily apply this yourself but it is messy, so either stand in the bath or on a sheet on the floor.

Pakistani massage paste Soak two handfuls of lentils in water overnight. Put these in the liquidizer with some milk and wash yourself with the resultant mixture. The mother of a friend of mine always uses this, and her skin has a luminous quality and is amazingly soft and clear. I often use this as well, and have converted some of my friends to it. Massage the paste into the skin just as you would use soap and then rinse off with warm water. Your skin will be shiny and smooth. Another way of using this mixture is to massage it in, and rub it off as it dries. It is a dramatic cleanser, as all the impurities and dirt come off with it, leaving the skin glowing, and immaculately clean. But only make a small quantity, as the mixture should be used fresh each time.

dough scrub I was most interested to read in an old book that the Nubians used dough for cleaning. In the last century an English consul in Berbia asked for a bath and a woman entered with a bowl of dough and a cup of scented oil. The dough was rubbed into his bare body to cleanse it thoroughly, after which the oil was applied to give elasticity to the limbs.

massage cream This is a fairly heavy and rich massage cream which will need to be rubbed in well. It will leave your skin feeling marvellously smooth because of all the lanolin.

4 tablespoons lanolin
4 tablespoons sunflower or safflower oil

9 tablespoons water

Perfume

Heat the oils together and then slowly add the heated water. Add a tablespoon of wintergreen or camphor oil to make a really invigorating massage cream which will be very good for aching muscles. But if you cannot bear the smell, decrease the amount of wintergreen or camphor and add an aromatic herb oil. These proportions make approximately one cup of rich, pale yellow cream. To make this cream lighter simply add 2 tablespoons of petroleum jelly.

½ cup almond oil
½ cup castor oil
1 teaspoon camphor oil

massage oil Mix all the oils together and use.

Body lotions

A princess, the daughter of Boabdil, Emir of Granada, in 1491,

used to make a body lotion out of boiled and crushed chestnuts, perfumed with musk. One evening, her maidservant, having fallen in love with a Spanish nobleman, suitor to the princess, kept tryst with him in the garden, dressed in one of the princess's robes, and scented with this body lotion. The nobleman, who had been jealous of the princess's interest in another lover, stabbed the girl and escaped over the wall. The princess, who had been hidden, revealed herself and managed to save the maidservant's life. An exemplary story, but this lotion is still used by the gypsies of Granada, who rub themselves all over with it before their wedding night. One young dancer called 'Silver Knees' told me the story when I visited Granada.

rose and lime body lotion Use this mixture after the bath if you suffer from dry skin. The marvellous thing about this lotion is that it is not oily and so you can get dressed straight away, without ruining your clothes. Try and persuade children with dry skin to use it – one friend of mine used it on her children and their skin was immensely improved.

3 tablespoons rosewater
1 tablespoon glycerine
2 tablespoons lime juice

Change the proportions of this lotion to suit your own skin, and mix it until the lotion no longer feels sticky and goes into your skin easily. The quantities given make about half a cup.

blue satin body lotion Put the soapflakes and water in a saucepan and heat. When the soapflakes are dissolved, remove from the heat and add the glycerine, olive oil and witch-hazel. Stir until cool and then add the blue colouring and some perfume (I use pine oil to make it invigorating). You now have about half a cup of a lovely thin, creamy blue mixture which makes an ideal, non-greasy, after-bath body lotion which leaves the skin feeling like satin.

4 tablespoons water
3 tablespoons soapflakes

1 teaspoon glycerine
1 teaspoon witch-hazel
4 teaspoons olive oil

Drop of blue colouring
Perfume

lavender body lotion Dissolve the borax in the rosewater, then slowly add the warmed oil, beating all the time. If you have an electric beater use that, if not, an egg beater. When all the oil has been added to the water and it forms an emulsion, add the lavender water. This is a thin lotion which softens the skin, suitable for both body and hands.

2 tablespoons olive, groundnut or safflower oil

1 cup rosewater
1 teaspoon borax

4 teaspoons lavender water

Lavender water is made by infusing a handful of lavender flowers in 2 cups of boiling water. Let this stand for an hour and then strain and use.

almond body lotion Heat the oils and waters in the usual way.

3 teaspoons lanolin
1 teaspoon almond oil
1 teaspoon petroleum jelly
1 teaspoon vegetable lard

2 teaspoons glycerine
10 tablespoons water
1 teaspoon soapflakes
1 teaspoon cornflour

Perfume (almond essence)

Remove them from the heat, and mix them together. Pour the mixture into a bottle and shake vigorously. Now add perfume. This makes about a cup of liquid lotion, which is non-greasy, and is absorbed into the skin straight away. Sometimes it has a slight tackiness when very first applied but this goes, leaving the skin with a really beautiful glowing sheen. One friend adds a teaspoon of honey to this lotion, which she finds ideal for her skin – so experiment to see what suits *you*.

'Her pure and eloquent blood
Spoke in her cheeks, and so distinctly wrought,
That one might almost say, her body thought.'
Donne

LOOKING BETTER THAN YOU FEEL

When you're tired or unwell, you are horribly conscious of looking as bad as, or worse than, you feel! When you are stuffed up with a cold, suffering from period pains, bored with pregnancy, or going through post-natal depression, it is wise to maintain your beauty routine. Looking better is such a booster to your morale that it often makes you feel instantly healthier.

Don't let your hair stay dirty: nothing is quite as demoralizing – or as unattractive – as lank and greasy hair. Even if you feel it's not wise or you can't manage to wash it, use one of the dry shampoos I mention in the hair section. And learn how to use scarves. They can be tied into all sorts of ingenious shapes and glamorous turbans which hide a multitude of sins – and as they look dramatic people will presume you look good!

One of the simplest ways of looking better immediately is a traditional part of the Japanese bride's wedding make-up; she puts pink on her eyelids to give her a delicate, youthful and blushing appearance. So when you feel ill, tired, or are just looking a bit pale, try some blusher on your eyelids and a little on your cheeks, and your face will instantly look healthier, younger and fresher. And don't forget the amazingly reviving and relaxing effect of a bath: try having the bath by candlelight which is instantly glamorizing and soothing. After a long warm soak, oil yourself all over with a scented lotion, and splash on lots of cologne or perfume. Then you'll feel relaxed, pampered, and should look much better.

Cold preventions

The 'common cold' is one of the most 'unbeautifying' conditions possible, and this recipe for its prevention is trusted implicitly by a Polish woman who makes it each year, as did her mother and grandmother before her. Half fill a large sweet jar with 'dry'

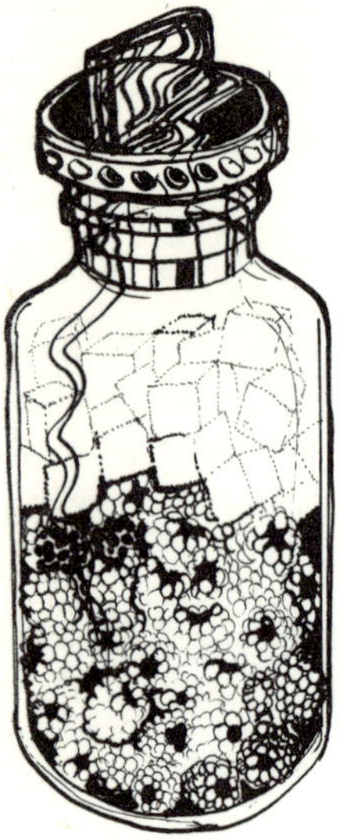

raspberries, and cover them, almost to the top of the jar, with hard sugar lumps. Screw the top on the jar and leave for several weeks. When the sugar has dissolved completely, add another fine layer of sugar lumps. When this has dissolved in turn, the juice is ready to be used. If you think you may be starting a cold, put a little raspberry juice into a glass of hot water. It tastes delicious and will practically always stop the cold in its initial stages. The juice stays fresh and will last several years.

Another recipe for preventing a cold is to make a very strong tea with peppermint. Drink this sweetened with honey throughout the day and even if the cold has in fact started, it will hasten your recovery and soothe you.

Another 'unlovely' thing is a cold or fever blister. If you suffer from these, next time you feel that itchy sensation heralding its arrival, cut a lemon and rub the area with the juice. Do this several times throughout the day and you will be amazed at how often it will prevent the blister forming. It is important, however, to catch the blister before it actually appears. Anyhow it is certainly worth trying.

Party pick-up

So often one comes home utterly exhausted after a long hard day, and it is just when we feel like that that we have to go out to a party or a rather important dinner date. After ploughing through rush-hour traffic it is often the last thing in the world we want to do. Next time it happens to you, try this simple thirty-minute pick-me-up.

1. First run a warm bath – don't make it too hot or you will end up with a bright red face (hot baths in any case, tend to make one sleepy which is not what you want now).

2. Now remove your makeup, if any.

3. Next your hair. If you're lucky it's all right, or you've got a wig, or you can cover it up with a turban. If not, you've got to do something fast. Put your hair into rollers and the steam from the bath will set it. I actually steam it with the kettle before getting into the bath (a well-known model taught me this trick) but it could be dangerous, so do please be careful. It does work, though, and is useful to remember for emergencies.

4. Now apply a mask to perk up your skin. If you have an egg in the kitchen, just whip it up with a few drops of oil and smear it over your face. It is slightly astringent, smoothing out and tight-

ening the skin, so before a party it is marvellous: just like an instant face lift.

5. All this should only have taken a few minutes and now you are ready to get into the bath. If you have a shower, a cold shower or even cold splash afterwards will really wake you up.

6. Then if you have enough time, go and lie down still with the mask on, and apply some eye pads. I use either cold tea bags, slices of cucumber, or best of all, thin slices of raw potato (see the *Eye* section for their various properties). Lie down with your feet higher than your head, turn on some soft music, and relax.

7. After about ten minutes, rinse off the mask, your skin will be transformed, and you should feel human again. As your skin now looks so clean and fresh you shouldn't need much make-up, which is another time-saver. Do your hair, and you'll be clean, refreshed, relaxed and beautiful, ready to face anything!

'A blemish in the soul cannot be corrected in the face; but a blemish in the face, if corrected, can refresh the soul.'

Cocteau

A HAPPY PERSON IS A BEAUTIFUL ONE!

It is said that when we frown we use forty-four muscles, and when we smile, only fourteen. Remembering this, I hope you enjoy making all these cosmetics. Not only should they help you look better, but if you're anything like me, you'll have such fun that your enjoyment will reflect in your face.

'Saints and Kings, prophets and Dervishes all bow down before beauty descending from the unknown world.
'We love beauty because it is not merely of this earth: beauty in the human being is a reflection of celestial beauty itself.'

Mahmud Shabistari
Secret Garden
Sufi Writings of the 13th century.

'Beauty is a promise of happiness.'
Stendhal

NOTES ON INGREDIENTS

Alcohol	Has antiseptic, preserving and grease-cutting properties. Used mainly in stimulating astringents and as a solvent for essential oils. In the USA you can buy pure ethanol alcohol, but in Britain you need a licence and so where any recipe specifies alcohol, substitute vodka.
Allantoin	A chemical from the herb, *Comfrey*. A water soluble anti-irritant with healing and soothing properties. It is added to many expensive products to help heal chapped skin and lips.
Almonds	Ground almonds are used extensively in the Middle East in face masks and as washing grains. Nourishing and cleansing.
Almond oil	A very fine rich oil. Used in preparations of all types.
Angelica	A herb which stimulates the skin. Used in the bath or in skin tonics.
Apples	A naturally acid fruit. Used in face masks and skin tonics.
Apple cider Vinegar	Restores the acid mantle to the skin. Can be used, diluted, as a skin tonic.
Apricots	Rich in Vitamin A. Use the pulp in face masks. Apricot oil is very rich in polyunsaturated oil so it is used in nourishing creams.
Alum	A fine white or yellow powder with astringent properties. Used in lotions and for hardening the feet. Also used as a dry shampoo to remove sweat and dirt.
Ascorbic acid	Vitamin C.
Avocado	Rich and nourishing with a high vitamin con-

tent. Use the pulp in feeding face masks and the oil in nourishing creams.

Baby oil	See *Mineral oil.*
Banana	Nourishing, used in masks.
Basil	Aromatic herb, used in infusions for tonics and the bath.
Beeswax	An ester-wax with a high melting point, ideal for face creams. An emulsifier when mixed with borax. (It takes eight pounds of honey to produce one pound of beeswax.)
Beer	Used to wash the face with or as a hair-setting lotion. In Uruguay the sediment from a beer factory is used by all the local women to wash with. It prevents skin rashes.
Benzoin	A balsamic resin from trees in Java, it has antiseptic and preserving properties. Tincture of benzoin is the liquid. Used in creams and skin tonics.
Benzoic acid	A preservative.
Bergamot	An aromatic herb.
Bergamot oil	A volatile oil expressed from the rind of the citrus bergamia. Used to perfume colognes and toilet waters, and also in minute quantities to help tanning.
Bicarbonate of soda	An acid salt of carbonic acid used for cosmetic purposes, to clean the teeth.
Blackberry juice	Healing, used to cure eczema. Blackberry leaves can be used in the bath for clearing the skin.
Borage	A flowering herb. An infusion of the flowers and leaves is used as an eye lotion.
Borax	Colourless transparent crystals which have mild detergent and antiseptic properties. Used as an emulsifier in conjunction with beeswax.
Bran	Used in bath-softening recipes or as a substitute for oatmeal in masks.
Brandy	See *Alcohol.*
Brewers' yeast	A rich source of Vitamin B and protein. Taken internally it helps acne and dryness of the skin and scalp. Powdered brewers' yeast is used in cleansing face masks.
Buttermilk	Used as a cleanser for bleaching slight discolora-

tion, especially on the neck. Widely used in the Middle East. Good for oily skins.

Cabbage	Use water it has been cooked in, for washing. Rich in vitamins and minerals.
Calamine lotion	An alkaline lotion used to soothe irritated skin. Contains lime water, glycerine, zinc oxide and calamine.
Calendula	See *Marigold.*
Camomile	The flowers of this herb are used for cleansing, soothing and bleaching. They make a very good hair rinse for fair hair (before bleaches were widely available all our grandmothers used camomile). Camomile skin tonic also has a marvellous reputation. Camomile tea reputedly cures hangovers.
Camphor	A white crystalline substance used as an antiseptic. It is healing and soothing when used on spots. Use either camphor cake or camphor spirit, but be sure to ask for camphor BP.
Camphor oil	Stimulating, and a rubefactant (it reddens the skin). Applied locally it warms and relieves aching muscles. Used in massage creams. I mix small amounts into my massage oil during winter to improve the circulation and give a warm sensation.
Carrots	Rich in Vitamin A. Use the pulp in a cleansing mask. Use carrot oil in nourishing eye creams, and the juice in face masks.
Castor oil	A rich oil, used especially in hair products.
Cocoa butter	Solidified waxy oil from the roasted cocoa bean, used as a lubricant in massage creams. Especially good for dry skin.
Coconut oil	Is used in face creams and on the hair. Nourishing.
Cod liver oil	Rich in vitamin D. Taken internally in tablet form, it improves dry skin.
Comfrey	A herb with healing and soothing properties, the source of *Allantoin.* Either liquidize and use the juice as a skin tonic, and the pulp as a face mask, or make an infusion and use that as a skin tonic. Marvellous for spotty or chapped skin, so never be without it.

Corn oil	A heavy vegetable oil which can be used in body and face creams.
Corn milk	Used on dry skin, rich in Vitamin A and magnesium.
Cream (double or single	Nourishing. Massage with it and use it in face masks.
Cloves	An aromatic spice. Used in skin tonics and stimulating face masks.
Cucumber	Slightly astringent, and always feels cool and refreshing. Used in lotions, creams and masks.
Dandelions	Rich in Vitamins A and C. Used as a face wash which is slightly bleaching. Good for pimples.
Dandelion leaves	Possess diuretic properties. Make an infusion of them and drink this tea once or twice a day.
Dried milk	Nourishing, used to thicken face masks.
Eggs	One of the oldest, most useful aids to beauty. The yolk is nourishing and the white is drying and tightening. Use in masks and hair conditioners.
Elderflowers	Are used extensively in skin tonics and creams because of their refreshing, cleansing and soothing qualities. Help keep skin free from spots.
Emulsifying wax B.P.	An emulsifying agent which is extremely useful for stabilizing creams. Made from ceto stearyl alcohol and sodium lauryl sulphate.
Eyebright	A herb used as an eye-wash.
Fennel	Is a herb which has a cleansing effect on the skin. Use it in the water when steaming your face or in skin tonics. Also reputed to help slimming.
Fuller's earth	An absorbent clay, rich in minerals. Used in face masks for thickening and for its cleansing, drawing, and stimulating qualities. Also used as a dry shampoo and foot powder.
Garlic	Antiseptic and drawing properties. Add a small amount to masks.
Gelatine	A rich source of protein. Use in hair conditioners or diluted as a setting lotion and in nail hardening creams. To strengthen nails take one tablespoon daily.

Glycerine — Use in face creams and lotions. A humecant, which means that it attracts and holds moisture. If too high a proportion is used it will absorb moisture from the skin, but used in moderation, it is very useful.

Grapes — Slightly acid, thus cleansing and bleaching. Use the pulp in masks and the juice in tonics.

Groundnut oil — A vegetable oil used in face creams and body lotions. Also known as peanut oil.

Gum resins — Gum arabic and mucilage of tragacanth are natural resins and are used as tightening, fixing and stabilizing agents in creams; can be dissolved in water.

Henna — An astringent herb with cooling properties; Oriental women apply it to their feet in paste form to cool a fever. It is also a very good hair dye, giving a strong auburn colour and conditioning the hair at the same time. The Arabs 'henna' the palms of their hands and feet and even use it as a nail dye.

Hollyhocks — Soothing properties. Make skin tonics from either, or both, the flowers and the leaves.

Honey — Healing, nourishing and softening. Used in masks, creams and lotions.

Hops — See *Beer*.

Houseleek — Herb used for healing and astringent properties in lotions.

Jasmine oil — An highly aromatic oil from the flower, used as perfume in many recipes.

Kaolin — A fine white clay used for absorption purposes in masks.

Kelp — Seaweed rich in minerals. Used in masks, especially good on greasy or spotty skins.

Kohl — A dark powder used by oriental women to outline their eyes.

Lanolin — A thick tacky fat from sheep's wool. A natural emollient and emulsifier which will absorb twice its weight of water. Widely used in skin foods for its moisturizing and softening effects. There are two types of lanolin – anhydrous which is thick

	and sticky and hydrous which has added water to it and so is lighter. I use anhydrous in my cosmetics.
Lavender	Known for its characteristic sweet smell which is used in perfumes. Used as a mouth wash to prevent bad breath.
Lecithin powder	A complex, highly nutritious soft yellow powder found in egg yolk and soya beans. Used in face masks and nourishing creams.
Lemon	Vitamin C. Lemon juice is acid, astringent and bleaching. Used in skin tonics and creams. Lemon essence commonly used to perfume cosmetics.
Lemon peel	Contains essential aromatic oils and small amounts of natural anti-oxidants. The ground peel is used in abrasive face-washing preparations or face masks.
Lemonbalm	A herb which is good for clearing the skin. Make an infusion with it and use as a face wash.
Lettuce	Lettuce leaves are rich in minerals, iron and vitamins. Use an infusion as a skin tonic. It is cooling, and excellent if you are sunburnt to reduce redness.
Liquid paraffin	See *Mineral oil.*
Marigold	Calendula. The mucilage in the flowers and leaves is very beneficial for clearing the skin of eczema, spots and grease. It is claimed to be rejuvenating.
Mayonnaise	Nourishing, used as a face mask or hair conditioner.
Melon	Used on dry skin for refreshing and cleansing the skin. The finely crushed seeds can be used in masks.
Milk	Used for softening, nourishing and cleansing the skin. It is a very effective cleanser. (A friend who makes leather goods uses milk to clean the leather of any spots and stains).
Mineral oil	A fine, colourless, non-penetrating oil which rests on top of the skin. Ideal for cleansing creams but not nearly as good as a vegetable oil for other creams, lotions and bath oils.
Mint	Stimulating and refreshing herb. Used in skin tonics and masks.

Mucilage of tragacanth	See *Gum resins.*
Musk	A strong smelling substance from a gland of the musk deer. Used to fix scents, ie to prevent the smell evaporating.
Myrrh	A resin used in incense. Added to skin tonics it has preservative and mild disinfectant properties. A few drops of tincture of myrrh added to water make a very good mouth-wash which is reported to cure ulcerated gums.
Nettles	A mildly astringent circulation booster. A strong infusion of nettle juice massaged into the scalp daily cures dandruff and increases growth of hair. A nettle infusion can also be used to wash with, to clear the complexion.
Nipagin M	A preservative. A couple of drops added to creams will give them a longer shelf life.
Oatmeal	A cleansing, soothing meal. Use it for washing with, or in masks. I use the finely ground oatmeal found in any grocer's shop.
Oleic acid	A most useful oily liquid which has emulsifying properties. If a cream or lotion is separating, add 1 or 2 drops of oleic acid to bind it together.
Olive oil	A polyunsaturated vegetable oil. Used in nourishing creams.
Onions	An antiseptic. Wash with onion juice to prevent blemishes. Some old recipes mix it with honey to make an anti-wrinkle cream.
Orange	Vitamin C, acidic fruit. The juice is used in skin tonics and masks.
Orange peel	Dry and grind some peel and use it in masks or facial scrubs. Also used in tooth powders.
Orange-flower water	A fragrant water produced by distilling orange blossom. Used in creams and tonics.
Papaya	Or paw-paw. Softening and cleansing. The enzymes in the fruit have a deep cleansing effect by breaking down the dead skin. In Africa it is used to tenderize tough meat!
Parsley	Contains Vitamin C; cuts down the oiliness of

	the skin. An infusion of parsley rubbed into the scalp each day helps cure dandruff. Can also be used in skin tonics or masks.
Peach	Moisturizing, nourishing and delicious smelling. Use the mashed pulp on dry, rough skin in creams, masks and tonics.
Peanut oil	See *Groundnut oil.*
Peppermint	Stimulating. Use peppermint extract for its tightening, stimulating effect in skin tonics and masks.
Petroleum jelly	A lubricating jelly often used in cleansing and hand and nail creams.
Pine	Put the needles in a muslin bag in the bath to refresh and soothe aching muscles. Pine oil can also be added to the bath.
Plum	Cleansing. Use the pulp of the ripe fruit in masks or the juice in tonics and creams.
Potatoes	Cleansing and 'drawing' properties. Clears the skin. Use thin raw potato slices for eye pads to remove puffiness from eyes.
Raspberries	Cleansing. Use the crushed fruit in masks or the juice in skin tonics.
Rosehips	Rich in Vitamin C. Use the juice in tonics; good for blemishes.
Rosemary	A highly aromatic herb; a healing, stimulating circulation booster. A strong infusion of rosemary is used on dark hair to darken it and stimulate its growth. Widely used in all cosmetics.
Rosewater	A scented water made from rose petals. Widely used in skin tonics and creams.
Rose oil	A highly aromatic essential oil widely used in all cosmetics.
Rhubarb	The root is used to lighten hair, gives a honey gold colour.
Safflower oil	A rich polyunsaturated oil, suitable for all nourishing cosmetics. Unfortunately it tends to go rancid if stored for too long, especially if exposed to the air. So keep it tightly capped.
Sage	An astringent herb, suitable for use on oily skins and large pores. Used in tooth powders. Or just rub a sage leaf over the teeth to clean them. As a

	final hair rinse used to darken and revitalize the hair.
Salt	Used mixed with equal parts of bicarbonate of soda as excellent tooth powder. Also used as an abrasive body rub to tone the skin and improve circulation. It is also used as a slight antiseptic.
Sesame oil	A polyunsaturated nut oil. Useful in all cosmetics, especially suntanning creams as it absorbs ultra-violet rays, thus shielding the skin from them.
Soapflakes	A soap solution used as an emulsifying agent.
Sodium sesqui carbonate	A powdery substance which is a water softener, and is used in bath salts.
Spermaceti	A white wax from whale sperm, which is often mentioned in old recipes. I replace it with either emulsifying wax, or lanette wax which I find more effective.
Storax	The resin from the plant styrax. It was used in medicines.
Stearic acid	A natural, fatty acid. It is a crystalline, white waxy substance, which gives pearliness to creams, especially used in hand and body creams.
Strawberries	The fruit is cleansing, good for removing discoloration and blemishes from the skin, and even for cleaning the teeth. A lotion made from the leaves is soothing when used as an eye lotion or on eczema.
Sugar	An abrasive face scrub. Lather the face with soap then add a handful of sugar and scrub; rinse off and apply lemon juice. This thoroughly cleanses and stimulates the skin.
Sulphur	A yellow powder used in acne preparations. It is said to help slow down the activity of the oil-producing glands. Some people are allergic to it, so before using it on your face, give yourself a skin test behind the ear.
Sunflower oil	Rich in polyunsaturates. Widely used in creams of all kinds.
Tarragon	An aromatic herb with a strong fresh smell. Used in skin tonics and lotions.

Tea — Contains tannin which has a soothing and healing effect. Tannin absorbs ultra violet light and so is used in sun creams to help prevent burning. Tea also soothes, and has been used for centuries on burns.

Tea bags — Make marvellous soothing ready-made eye pads.

Thyme — A soothing herb used in skin tonics, for face steaming, and in baths.

Tomato — A slightly acidic fruit containing potassium and Vitamin C. Use it on blackheads, open pores and greasy skin.

Turnips — Have 'drawing' properties; use either raw, grated or boiled in cleansing masks.

Turtle oil — Vitamin enriched oil. Often used in rich nourishing creams. Very effective but unfortunately smells rather strong.

Vaseline — See *Petroleum jelly*.

Vinegar — Acid. Use diluted 8 parts water to 1 part vinegar to restore the acid mantle to the skin. If you suffer from itchy skin use it in the bath, and it will not only cure it but also improve and soften the skin.

Vitamins — A. Can pass through the skin, and so is valuable for use in dry skin and acne creams. Said also to have soothing properties.

B. Taken internally, this is said to promote health of skin and hair.

C. Is said to pass through the skin's surface and promote healing. Used in burn and acne creams.

D. Can be absorbed through the skin and has a healing effect on the skin, especially when combined with Vitamin A.

E. Said to have healing properties.

F. Counteracts dry, chapped skin; greatly used in face and hand creams. It is also used in hair treatments to counteract brittle hair.

Water — Very important as most creams have over 30% water. Light fluffy creams and cleansing lotions can have as much as 80% water. If possible use purified or at least boiled water when making cosmetics, as this helps prevent bacteria.

Drinking lots of water is a marvellous beauty recipe for the skin, helping to keep it clear of blemishes.

Wheatgerm flour Use it mixed with double cream to massage the body. Cleansing and softening.

Wheatgerm oil A rich unsaturated oil, rich in Vitamin E. Has healing properties.

Witch-hazel Made from twigs of the hamamelis or alder bush. Widely used in skin tonics for its astringent properties.

Yarrow A herb said to have healing properties.

Yeast See *Brewers' yeast*.

Yoghourt A fermented liquor made from milk. Natural yoghourt contains enzymes. Used as a base for cleansing and cleaning face masks.

Zinc oxide A heavy white powder. It has mildly astringent and antiseptic properties. Used as a dusting powder or mixed with benzoated lard to make a soothing ointment. Calamine lotion contains a small amount of zinc oxide.

'She walks in beauty, like the night
Of cloudless climes and starry skies;
And all that's best of dark and bright
Meet in her aspect and her eyes.'

Lord Byron

INDEX

N

O

P

R